★ A Populist Manifesto
The Making of a New Majority

★ A Populist Manifesto
The Making of a New Majority

★ by Jack Newfield and Jeff Greenfield

★ Praeger Publishers
New York · Washington

BOOKS THAT MATTER

Published in the United States of America in 1972
by Praeger Publishers, Inc.
111 Fourth Avenue, New York, N.Y. 10003

Library of Congress Catalog Card Number: 71–181695

Printed in the United States of America

This one is for Robert Kennedy

★ Contents

Preface   ix

Part One   A New Coalition—An Old Tradition

1 The New Populism   3
2 A Disrupted History   14

Part Two   The Issues—and the Programs

3 Concentrated Economic Power   33
4 The Money Changers: Banking and Insurance   51
5 Natural Monopolies, Unnatural Profits: Utilities   67
6 Them That Has, Keep: Taxes   89
7 The Great American Dream Machine: Regulatory
  Agencies   103
8 This Land Is Their Land: Land Reform   111
9 What They Say Is What You Get: The Media   120
10 The Great Cop-Out: Crime   133
11 The Medical-Industrial Complex: Health   148
12 Labor Pains: Unions and Work   162
13 Fight Fiercely, Harvard: Foreign Policy   175
14 Opening Up the Political Process   186

Part Three   A New Majority for Justice

15 The Making of a New Majority   203
A Final Word   219

★ Preface

THIS MANIFESTO is a platform for a movement that does not yet exist. It is not a book about the 1972 campaign, or a blueprint for Utopia in 2001.

It is instead an effort to return to American politics the economic passions jettisoned a generation ago. Its fundamental argument is wholly unoriginal: some institutions and people have too much money and power, most people have too little, and the first priority of politics must be to redress that imbalance.

For the past two decades, most of conservative politics has been based on fear—fear of Communists, fear of blacks, fear of crime. We believe the only antidote to fear, the only thing deeper than fear, is self-interest. Thus, the political appeal of the program we suggest in this manifesto is based not on moralistic or humanitarian grounds, but on pure self-interest.

Our analysis spans both conventional politics and extra-electoral movements. Its rests on ideas and trends that will grow and converge throughout the decade. Its evidence is drawn largely from the separate investigations of men and women, some of whom would disagree with our politics. But we believe that, taken together, the facts of economic and political life point to the need for redistribution.

We recognize the danger that populism may become a political fad, like hot pants or astrology, bursting into the speeches of dozens of candidates, and then vanishing. It is one of the depressing characteristics of America that an idea can travel from the underground, to showbiz popularity, to nostalgia in six months.* And we can already hear the most venal of politicians call themselves "populist," even as they cast their secret committee votes for every special interest in sight. There is nothing we can do about that, barring a political Truth-in-Labeling Act, except to suggest the issues by which an impostor can be measured.

We also recognize the limits of populism. History offers an unsettling number of examples where politicians railed against the economically privileged while at the same time building up hysteria against blacks, Jews, Catholics, and immigrants. We concede that a populist movement could flourish while ignoring or belittling the legitimate grievances of blacks, or the women's movement. All we can say is that a movement which ignores such groups is not authentic. We acknowledge, also, that populism has only a marginal impact on the vital questions of civil liberties, disarmament, and ecology. This is a manifesto designed to move us closer toward justice, not Shangri-la.

In the spirit of the British parliamentary practice of "declar-

---

* In the few months between the conception and completion of this book, the first modern "official" populist candidate for President—Oklahoma Senator Fred Harris—declared and withdrew from the race. This demonstrates several things worth remembering about politics: first, that some good causes lose; second, that a public figure cannot incarnate himself as a "populist" or anything else without years of visible, tough work—people might have responded more enthusiastically had they seen and heard Fred Harris fighting corporate America on a continuing basis in the Senate for six years; third, that big campaign contributors do not readily back the campaign of a man who is out to reduce their wealth and power.

ing our interest," we acknowledge that our proposals to redistribute wealth and power will cost us personally: both of
us have comfortable incomes, both of us have access to people
with power. But we are prepared as individual citizens to pay
more taxes, to have less money to spend, if a fairer amount
of funds can be spent on redeeming America and healing
our countrymen.

This book is not a bible. We might well be wrong about
some of our beliefs; indeed, we have changed some of our
opinions in the process of writing this book. But we hope it is
a beginning.

Finally, we wish to acknowledge the intellectual debt we
owe to several people, some of whom we have disagreed with
in the past, some of whom we have never met, some of whom
are good friends:

Gus Tyler, C. Wright Mills, Studs Terkel, Mike Harrington,
Harvey Swados, Nick Pileggi, Brendan Sexton, Howard Zinn,
Christopher Lasch, Pete Hamill, Jimmy Breslin, Robert Coles,
Adam Walinsky, Anthony Mazzochi, Paul DuBrul, David
Mixner, Peter Barnes, and Vic Reinemer.

Thanks too to Clay Felker and *New York Magazine* for
publishing the original article that led to this book.

And last, thanks to our editor, Marian Wood, for restoring
our faith in the publishing business.

JACK NEWFIELD
JEFF GREENFIELD

Part One ★ A New Coalition–
An Old Tradition

1 ★ The New Populism

THE AMERICAN myth is dying. Things are not getting better. Instead, history seems deranged. We have lost our way.

The Kennedys and King, Evers and Malcolm X are murdered in public, while our sons march off to war, and we watch them burn Ben Tre in our living rooms. Pentagon documents reveal our leaders were liars; our sons come back with track marks on their arms, and throw their Purple Hearts over the White House Wall.

"Things fall apart/the center cannot hold" is true of products and neighborhoods and our moral universe. Our cars can kill; cans of soup are lethal; the telephone breaks down. So does the city's electricity. So do the links between parents and children. The neighborhood of a lifetime imprisons its elderly in their apartments after sunset. And their predators are themselves imprisoned by the heroin in their blood. There is desolation in Eastern Kentucky, where men in their forties look for work that is not there and die of black lung. In Brownsville, Sutter Avenue looks like a moonscape. A geog-

3

raphy is drawn in blood: Birmingham, My Lai, Attica, Dallas, Kent State, the Ia Drang Valley.

These are differing evils. But if there is a unified sense of discontent, some impulse to which most Americans would assent, it is that we have lost the power to alter our society because those with power are exempt from accountability. This sensibility—which strikes to the core of America's foundations—has poisoned the wellsprings of trust. "The rich get richer and the poor get poorer." So 62 per cent of white America tell the Harris Poll. "The medium is a false message." So the Vice-President tells the American people. A quarter of the American people abandoned their trust in our government between 1964 and 1970; by the start of this decade, two-thirds of us believed we had lost our national sense of direction; half of us thought we were on the verge of a national breakdown. If a presidential aspirant preaches war, and you vote for the man who promises peace, you have been duped; for the peacemaker has all along been plotting war—and lies to win your assent to that war. So the Pentagon papers tell us.

Nor is it just the government we have come to doubt. By one measure—a Harris Poll in September of 1971—*every major institution in America* was distrusted by a majority of Americans. The press, business, the courts, Congress, the media, the presidency—*none* of them commanded the respect of the citizenry.

And thus millions of citizens have come to believe that the men and institutions who hold power in this country do not mean what they say: that the Constitution, or a hospital bill, or the label on a can of food, or a *Time* magazine story, or a union pension plan, all falter between the word and the deed. The institutions that govern us—from the presidency to a corporation to a university, a bank, a foundation—do not deserve the legitimacy that is supposed to come with authority. They endure not because they fulfill their purposes, but because they possess power.

This belief is not unique to any single group of Americans.

It cuts across divisions of race, sex, class, age, and region. We are infested with the proposition that the rules of the game are not fair; that the fight is fixed; that the key to success in America is power, and that the key to power is the hidden angle, the fix, money.

The core of this manifesto lies in this perception: there are people, classes, and institutions that today possess an illegiti-mate amount of wealth and power; they use that power for their own benefit and for the common loss. This power, which is at root economic, corrupts the political process and insulates itself from effective challenge.

The fight against this concentration of privilege—open and covert, legal and illegal—is, we believe, the most important political question of this decade. Its goal is a more equitable distribution of wealth and power; its enemy is the entire arrangement of privileges, exemptions, and free rides that has narrowed the opportunity of most Americans to control their own destiny. This fight for fairness is political; it can be won only by organizing a new political majority in America.

There exists a 200-year-old native tradition behind this goal of fairness and equality. It is a tradition that stretches back to Jefferson and Tom Paine, to Andrew Jackson, the muckrakers, George Norris, and Robert La Follette; it runs through the early organizers of the CIO and the political battles of Estes Kefauver; and it comes down to us today in the campaigns and ideas of Martin Luther King, Robert Kennedy, and Ralph Nader. It is called populism. We believe that a new populism, stripped of the paranoia and racism that afflicted it in the past, can redress some of the key grievances that have stunted the lives of millions of us. It is a *political* movement with a *political* goal. It is *not* a cultural prescription or a revolutionary nostrum. Far from being a Utopian dream, the new populism rests on a new majority that is, we believe, both a necessary and an attainable coalition. It is also the most important work we have.

Three essential beliefs govern this manifesto, and we state them bluntly at the outset.

ONE   **Wealth and power are unequally and unfairly distributed in America today**

After a generation of predominantly liberal, predominantly reformist national governments, the concentration of wealth has *increased*. In 1949, the richest 1 per cent of the population owned 21 per cent of the wealth. Today, the richest 1 per cent own almost 40 per cent of our national wealth. Income distribution has not changed for a generation: the bottom fifth of American families gets 6 per cent of the national income; the top fifth gets 40 per cent.

This wealth is shielded by private corporate governments, which are themselves protected by the political process their wealth helps shape.* These are the corporate enterprises that pervade our society: General Motors and First National City Bank, the National Broadcasting Company and Columbia University, the American Medical Association and the AFL-CIO, Getty Oil and AT&T. These institutions are often at odds with each other; they often favor different aspirants to national power and prefer different national priorities. But each holds basic, sometimes life and death, power over the millions of individuals whose lives they touch; each of them maintains this power no matter who is elected to public office; and each believes, first and foremost, in self-perpetuation and aggrandizement—regardless of what that means for public policy.

These epicenters of power do not win every battle with the public: auto safety laws are sometimes passed, utility rate

---

* So that we have Henry Jackson, whose servility to the biggest aerospace company in his state has won him the title of "Senator from Boeing"; and Russell Long, who inherited his role as protector of the oil industry when Robert Kerr died and Lyndon Johnson left the Senate; and Congressman Jamie Whitten, who is the spokesman for the big corporate farmers. And so on.

increases are occasionally denied. But as a general proposition, these groups possess the power to govern themselves and to affect the whole society, and this power is beyond the reach of public or individual redress. No individual who works for a living can avoid taxes; Atlantic Richfield Oil Company paid no taxes for four years although it earned $465 million during that period. No homeowner could hurl his garbage into the street because it hurt his family budget to buy a trash can; the U.S. Steel Corporation has turned Gary, Indiana and countless other communities into open sewers. If a motorist is caught speeding and offers money to the traffic cop, he is guilty of bribery; if doctors are caught participating in the padding of Medicare bills and the AMA spends thousands to stop Congress from legislating reform, it is engaging in public-service advertising.* This imbalance of power is not the result of a conspiracy: such institutions are simply using the power they have to preserve their privileged status in the American hierarchy.

As city planner Charles Abrams first suggested, our economic system is best described as welfare for the rich and free enterprise for the poor. There are $4 billion in federal subsidies every year for big corporate farmers; there are depletion allowances and import quotas to enrich the oil industry; there are expense-account dodges, untaxed foreign bank accounts, and special exemptions for the income from stocks and bonds —all for the rich. Both big business and big labor organizations can hire lobbyists, raise money for political campaigns, and lend out their employees to candidates while keeping them on tax-deductible salaries. The biggest defense contractors—General Dynamics, Lockheed, Boeing—have been virtually subsidized by the Pentagon, as have elitist "think-tanks"

---

* A view certainly held officially. Despite intensive political lobbying by the AMA, the IRS continues to recognize the organization's tax-exempt status for most of its revenues; yet, the Sierra Club had its exemption challenged ostensibly for just such activities.

such as the RAND Corporation.* And the tax system is itself a major subsidy to the wealthy.

Meanwhile, the billions of dollars spent as a result of the reform legislation of the Truman, Kennedy, and Johnson years—on such items as urban renewal, Medicare, the $60 billion highway construction program, the War on Poverty, and aid to education—have made little difference for the forgotten families living on less than $10,000 a year. Administrators profited from these programs, politicians and consultants profited, construction firms profited, but the poor and the nonaffluent did not.

And it is not just blacks or Chicanos or Indians who are victimized by our double-standard economy. Nor is it only those on the poverty level. The majority of Americans are victimized.

White factory workers in Birmingham and Flint still lead frustrated, dead-end lives: the average worker's income is $1,000 less than the Department of Labor says he needs to take care of a family of four, and more often than not his wife also works at a dull, unrewarding job that is nonetheless essential if the family is to make ends meet. The waitress in Cleveland still can't pay her mother's hospital bills, and the law still says her income makes her ineligible for public heath care. Old people living on Social Security still have to shoplift cans of tunafish so they can eat. And in New York City, the gross income of 60 per cent of white families is less than $9,400 a year—less, in other words, than a moderate standard of living. So much for the affluent society.

In his famous 1962 commencement address at Yale, President Kennedy argued that the crucial problems of the economy were no longer political or distributive, but had become managerial and technical. We argue the exact opposite.

* As a result of congressional action in 1971, "virtually" and "Pentagon" are no longer necessary modifiers in the case of Lockheed. Now, direct subsidization is the rule. And, in announcing his import surtax in August, 1971, Mr. Nixon specifically exempted Lockheed from its application—another form of subsidy.

TWO The key to building any new majority in American politics is a coalition of self-interest between blacks and low- and moderate-income whites; the real division in this country is not between generations or between races, but between the rich who have power and those blacks and whites who have neither power nor property

Until recently, such an alliance seemed impossible, in part because middle-class liberals have persistently defined public issues primarily in terms of race rather than class. "White racism," the Kerner Commission said, was the core of the problem. The OEO bureaucrats did not start any legal-services storefronts in the white sections of Youngstown or South Boston. There were no Model City grants to rebuild the decaying white neighborhoods of Utica or Jersey City. Affluent liberals, living safely behind suburban fences, refused to recognize street crime as an injustice against the old and the poor still trapped in the cities. Middle-class reformers sent their own children to "smart" private schools, and then supported plans that forced white ethnics to bus their children to predominantly black schools where education was inferior. By promising and not delivering to the blacks, and by ignoring the blue-collar worker, the liberals in power during the 1960's managed to anger and polarize both halves of the other America.

But blacks and millions of white workingmen who earn between $5,000 and $10,000 a year do have common problems and share common interests. To get them to recognize this and to act requires that these mutual needs become clearly defined and that programs to meet these needs be offered— *all in terms that benefit both groups.* Despite all the ethnic and racial divisions, blue-collar workers were progressive during the 1930's and 1940's. There is no reason why they can't be again.

We have already noted some of the issues than can unite them. As for the programs, a unifying populist platform might include: stricter industrial safety laws; a 90 per cent tax on inheritance and estates—and tax reforms to help the workingman; free medical care for everyone; public ownership of utilities; limits on land ownership by individuals and corporations; new antitrust laws to go after industrial concentration as well as monopoly; expanded Social Security benefits, including a decent income base for those who cannot work; cable television franchises for civic groups; free and equal access to television for all politicians; strict controls on the profits of banks; and an end to corporate power and control of both the market and the regulatory agencies.

The prospect for this new coalition appears uncertain today. Working-class whites and blacks are separate armed camps in Cicero, Illinois; school buses are bombed in Pontiac, Michigan, in an effort to halt racial busing. In 1968, New York watched as teachers—mostly Jewish—battled parents' groups—mostly black and Puerto Rican—for control of the city's schools. In public universities, on civil-service job lists, in housing, blacks and working-class whites collide, in large part because they are forced to compete against each other for what are, but need not be, inadequate resources. The result is distrust and hostility.

We do not argue that these disputes can be eradicated; racial and cultural hostilities are a fact of life. But we do argue that this competition is in part a consequence of economic concentration—concentration that leaves whites and blacks competing over too scarce public resources. We believe that a redistribution of wealth and power would diminish this combat that turns potential class allies into racial antagonists. If white and black communications workers find wages and promotions inadequate, whom should they blame? Each other? Or the conglomerate International Telephone and Telegraph that turned a profit of $350 million in 1970, and paid its board chairman, Harold Geneen, an annual compensation of $766,000? (Which is more than most Americans earn in a lifetime.) If white and black families are forced to compete against each other for decent housing at a fair price, whom should they blame? Each other? Or banks and insurance companies that finance a glut of new office buildings and luxury apartments and allow realty interests to make a profit out of slum housing?

Blacks and almost-poor whites do not have to love, or even like, each other to forge an alliance of self-interest. The Irish cop on the low end of the middle-income scale living in Brooklyn's Bay Ridge need not embrace the black family in Harlem or the Italian-American homeowner in Corona to know his kids are stuck with the same bad schools, dirty streets, and dangerous parks. The white miner in West Virginia and the Mexican-American migrant worker in Texas share a more important bond than friendship: because they and their families cannot get decent medical care, they will die younger, suffer more disease, and lose more children at birth. In short, the coalition we are describing is based on hard, practical politics. In 1932, Jewish trade unionists and southern segregationists did not love each other, but together they gave ballast to FDR's New Deal. Certainly the jobless youth in Watts and the steelworker laid off his job in Gary have more in common than antilabor millionaires like Senators James Buckley and William Brock III have in common with those blue-collar workers who voted for them.

In 1968, Robert Kennedy, an earthy enemy of war, hunger, and crime, won the votes of both blacks and ethnic whites who had been tempted to follow George Wallace. The organizing work of Saul Alinsky, Ralph Nader, and Msgr. Geno Baroni also indicates the existing potential for this alliance. So do the decisive electoral victories achieved in 1970 by Senators Hart, Proxmire, and Kennedy, by Governor Gilligan, and by Representatives Dellums and Abzug, and the 1971 election of independent populist Henry Howell as Virginia's Lieutenant Governor.

Once cemented, this pact between the have-nots could transform American politics. With the added weight of the burgeoning consumer, environmental, and women's movements, and the millions of new voters between eighteen and twenty-one, an effective political coalition could take power.

THREE **Conceptually and historically, the new populism differs from both the New Frontier and the New Left; it is a synthesis of many radical and some conservative ideas**

The new populism differs from the New Frontier in several distinctive and significant ways. First, it is a *movement*, a broad popular upsurge like the labor movement of the 1930's or today's antiwar movement; it is not a faction yoked to one political party or one charismatic personality. The new populist movement sees winning elections as only half the job because so much power is still locked beyond the reach of the democratic process. It mistrusts the technocrats from the RAND Corporation and the Harvard Business School. It is decentralist and participatory, believing change is generated from below. And, like most of the original populists, it is anti-imperialist in foreign policy.

At the same time, it understands that the New Left in its Weatherman, Panther, and Yippie incarnations has become antidemocratic, terroristic, dogmatic, stoned on rhetoric, and badly disconnected from everyday reality.

The new populism also recognizes that conservatives have been perceptive about such things as the menace of violent street crime, the failure of the welfare system, and the limits human nature places on the abilities of centralized government. Conservatives have been right, too, in sensing the country has lost contact with those human values the ethnic workingman prizes most: family, hard work, pride, loyalty, endurance.

Our basic argument in this manifesto is neither new nor novel. If it seems new, that is because over the last twenty years liberalism lost its vision and its memory, its élan and its program.

For a generation we have watched liberals gain more power and display less liberalism. It began in the early 1950's as liberal politicians and intellectuals dropped everything else to prove their anticommunism. Later in the decade, exhaustion and boredom set in, and political issues were subordinated to sociological concerns with affluence, organization men, suburbia, and mass culture. "The end of ideology" became an intellectual cliché.

During the Kennedy years, an eerie infatuation with management techniques and budgeting expertise—exemplified by Robert McNamara—became the new fashion. Increasingly divorced from a concern with programs, liberals turned these technocratic means into ends, ultimately chaining us by default to a set of distorted policies. So we became mired in a war begun by the anticommunists and the technocrats, and, since 1965, all our energies have of necessity been aimed at ending that war.

But now it is time to return again to the first questions of politics: who holds power—and by what right?

2 ★ A Disrupted History

THE HISTORY of populist reform is a history disrupted a generation ago and, except for a handful of isolated crusaders, never renewed.

For 150 years, the challenge to entrenched wealth was the cutting edge of insurgent politics. But after 1948, reform lost its memory and its will. Liberal politicians and intellectuals, grown complacent as their intentions turned into laws and programs, accepted the existing distribution of wealth in America. Economic manipulation of the corporate state became the political battleground—but the corporate state itself was accepted as necessary, benevolent, and immutable. The labor unions repudiated their strains of radicalism—and the AFL-CIO enlisted enthusiastically in the cold war. Ideology was pronounced dead; outrage old-fashioned.

Technocrats gained bureaucratic power, and brought to their jobs the theory that economic and political problems could be solved by computers and cost accountants. And, in a final irony, liberalism became elitist; a necessary accessory of fashion, coupled with indifference to the discontents of the

14

working class. The causes of the distant and exotic dispossessed preoccupied the Hamptons and Beverly Hills; while
the real afflictions of the working-class American—crime,
threats to job security, economic frustration, a loss of property
values, and the shredding of the social fabric—were shrugged
off as racist-motivated. So ironically, when blue-collar frus-
trations turned to rage and exploded onto the streets in 1970,
construction workers would march through Wall Street proclaiming "God Bless the Establishment."

As first Adlai Stevenson and then John Kennedy became
the symbols of liberal politics, Style became everything. And,
until he was brought down by the Vietnam War, Lyndon
Johnson could be hailed as a fighting liberal while steadfastly
protesting the economic privileges of Big Business.

This, then, is the central problem with the last twenty-five
years of American politics: *not that the country has grown
more conservative, but that liberalism has grown more conservative.*

Wealth tends to corrupt the mind and to nourish its love of
power, and to stimulate it to oppression. History proves this
to be the spirit of the opulent.—GOUVERNEUR MORRIS, *a
leader of the American aristocracy, at the Constitutional
Convention*

In a sense, the American nation was born to protect wealth
and power. The men who wrote the Constitution were brilliant
political thinkers and statesmen; but they were also land and
slave owners. They were determined to protect their interests
from attack at the hands of a propertyless mob; determined
to ensure that such a mob would never seize control of the
government. From Washington to Elbridge Gerry, a basic
distrust and fear of the people was explicit in their attempts
to create a self-limiting government. Indeed, one of the

Founding Fathers, Charles Pinckney, proposed that no one should be President who was not worth $100,000—a condition refused by his colleagues, but adopted by current realities.

All through the next 150 years, the fight to restrain wealth and power was a major, often decisive political battle. It seems hard to imagine in the face of today's politics of image and posture, but the fight against the excesses of capitalism was a political rallying cry for much of this country's history.

Much of Andrew Jackson's political movement was based on attacking economic monopolies given to the wealthy by Congress and the state legislatures. "The planter, the farmer, the mechanic, and the laborer," Jackson argued, were "in constant danger of losing their fair interest in the Government [to] the moneyed interests." In his veto of the National Bank, seen as a tool to enrich the prosperous, President Jackson set down this challenge:

> It is to be regretted that the rich and powerful too often bend the acts of government to their selfish purposes. [Inequality is inevitable]; but when the laws undertake to add to these natural and just advantages artificial distinctions, to grant titles, gratuities and exclusive privileges, to make the rich richer and the potent more powerful, the humble members of society—the farmers, mechanics, and laborers—who have neither the time nor the means of securing like favors to themselves, have a right to complain of the injustice of their government.

On the opposite side, arguing for the protected inequality of classes, John C. Calhoun anticipated Karl Marx in his insistence that all history broke down into the exploited and the exploiter. There never existed, he argued, "a wealthy and civilized community in which one portion did not live on the labor of another . . . the form in which slavery exists in the South is . . . but one modification of this condition." Just as Calhoun saw slavery and wage exploitation as part of the same process, so—at the Labor-Reform Convention of 1871

—Wendell Phillips, the greatest of the abolitionists and, by the end of his life, a prophetic champion of the labor movement, called for "war with the present system of finance, which robs labor and gorges capital, makes the rich richer and the poor poorer, and turns a republic into an aristocracy of capital."

But it was toward the end of the nineteenth century, with the concentration of power in private corporate leviathans, that the political hunger for reform crystallized in the populist movement. The rise of trusts and combines had put a few "robber barons" in total control of the lives of millions of Americans—and the rich had bribed legislators and congressmen with everything from free railroad passes to cash and stock to protect wealth from government control. Farmers found themselves forced to ship their produce on monopoly railroads at outrageous charges, or let their goods rot. Labor found itself forced to work in wretched conditions for almost nothing, and to be cheated by the "company stores," which were often the only places a miner or worker could buy food and clothing.

The result was the growth of populism—a remarkably mixed bag of eccentrics and prophets. There was much that was wrong with the People's Party and its leaders: conspiracy theories, rather than economic analysis, sometimes fueled their indignation; provincialism and paranoia were endemic; the fear of eastern combines had echoes of anti-Semitism, anti-Catholicism, and nativism. In the South, the original fusion of poor whites and poor blacks advocated by Georgia's Tom Watson turned ugly after Watson, repeatedly robbed of the congressional seat he had legitimately won, was driven by outrage and madness into violent racism. But, in 1892, Watson could tell his constituents:

Now the People's Party says to these two men [the black and the white farmer] "You are kept apart that you may be separately fleeced of your earnings. You are made to hate each other because upon that hatred is rested the keystone of the arch of financial despotism which enslaves you both. You are deceived and blinded that you may not see how this race antagonism perpetuates a monetary system which beggars both."

Within five years, Watson was leading night riders against black citizens.

Other parts of the populist program were equally ahead of their time—even Watson's early career anticipated a kind of southern politics that is only now beginning to emerge. The populists' 1892 platform warned against corporate monopolies, called for the nationalization of banks, utilities, and railroads, and urged redistribution of land; it endorsed the graduated income tax, direct elections of senators, and women's suffrage.

Today, the populists are seen largely as a quirk—a collection of Luddites with a dash of madness thrown in. Historian Richard Hofstadter, in his book *The Age of Reform,* wrote that "The Utopia of the Populists was in the past, not the future . . . they looked backward with longing to the lost agrarian Eden." Emphasizing the irrational aspect of the movement, Hofstadter claimed its true modern followers were Father Coughlin (the radio priest who began as a foe of economic privilege and ended his career as a confirmed anti-Semite and pro-Nazi), Huey Long, and Joe McCarthy. (Almost certainly, he would have added George Wallace.)

Our view, however, is closer to C. Vann Woodward's:

From many points of view the New Deal was neo-Populism. . . . The Populist doctrine of harmony of interest between farmer and labor, between workers and small businessmen, and the alignment of these "producers" against the parasitic "non-producers" is not without precedent in our political history. Any party that aspires to gain power in America must strive for a coalition of conflicting interest groups. The

Populist effort was no more irrational in this respect than was the Whig coalition and many others, including the New Deal.

Much of the energy of populism was deflected into the losing campaign of William Jennings Bryan and "free silver" in 1896, and, as an organized party, it had ceased to exist by the turn of the century. Yet the reforms for which it fought remained living causes, and even as the party was dying a new reform upsurge, ignited by muckraking journalists, was beginning. The work of Ida Tarbell, Lincoln Steffens, Gustavus Myers, Upton Sinclair, and Ray Stannard Baker all contained the essential populist insight that private corporate power was the enemy of citizen democracy.

Tarbell's careful series on Standard Oil, the biggest of all the trusts, led to its being broken up by Theodore Roosevelt. Sinclair's chilling novelistic account of the meatpacking industry (*The Jungle*) contributed to passage of the Pure Food and Drug Act. Steffens' exposés of urban political corruption (*The Shame of the Cities*) fueled a reform movement that was to have major consequences.

The vehicle for most of the muckrakers were national magazines with urban, middle-class readerships: *McClure's, American Magazine, Hampton's, Arena, Cosmopolitan.* The tradition ebbed after 1912 for a variety of reasons. The looming war in Europe, exhaustion of some of the writers, a failure to carry exposure into analysis and direct action, and the fact financial interests brought increasing pressure to bear—and even managed to gain control of *Hampton's* in 1911 and fire its crusading publisher, B. H. Hampton—served to undermine the muckraking thrust.

Paralleling the era of muckraking journalism was the Progressive movement, which was to reach its reforming apex in the 1924 presidential campaign of Wisconsin Senator Robert La Follette. The Progressive movement of the 1910's and 1920's, coming during a time of prosperity for all but the nation's farmers, put its emphasis on democratizing the political process and warned, in the words of Louis Brandeis, "against the curse of bigness" in the economy. Its targets were all forms of monopolistic control and its specific programs ranged from farmer credit unions to fair labor practice laws—including more humane treatment of industrial workers. In a sense, it was the link between the old populism and the New Deal.

When it arrived, the New Deal seemed at first to be a synthesis of fifty years of populist agitation. Kansas populist Sockless Jerry Simpson had attacked the "robber barons." Robert La Follette had attacked the "plutocrats." And FDR attacked the "economic royalists." In his first inaugural address, Roosevelt sounded like Bryan: "The money changers have fled from their high seats in the temple of our civilization. We may now restore that temple to the ancient truths."

The New Deal in power, however, was ambiguous, contradictory, and soon to split into rival factions: a radical camp (Harold Ickes, Rexford Tugwell, Robert Wagner, Sr.) and a conservative camp (James Farley, Raymond Moley, Henry Morgenthau).

In the end, its monuments of economic reform were considerable: a minimum wage law, Social Security, TVA, industrial union recognition, public housing, federal agencies to regulate the corporate economy. These accomplishments cannot be dismissed as marginal. But, when it was all over, the New Deal still left 20 to 30 million citizens living in poverty, and the giant corporations, swollen in power as a result of the war, were bigger and stronger than ever. Blacks still lived in ghettos and held the lowest-paying jobs. The New Deal did not find a durable way to redistribute the abundance of America, although it did try.

In 1948, Harry Truman waged his "give 'em hell," Cinderella campaign; it was to be the last presidential campaign in the populist tradition. Truman's temperament and oratory were all flavored with the old spirit. More important, so were elements of his program.

In January of 1948, Truman asked Congress to pass his "poor man's tax reduction" of $3.2 billion. He also introduced legislation for national health insurance, an extension of Social Security and unemployment benefits, and new civil rights and minimum wage laws. In April, Truman vetoed what he called "the rich man's tax bill" that Congress had enacted in place of his own. Also vetoed was the Taft-Hartley Act, which Truman attacked as being anti-union. It was on these bread-and-butter issues that Truman anchored his underdog campaign against Tom Dewey.

The basic Truman stump speech in 1948 went something like this:

> Republicans in Washington have a habit of becoming curiously deaf to the voice of the people. But they have no trouble hearing what Wall Street is saying. They are able to catch the slightest hint from Big Business.
>
> When I talk to you here today about the Republicans, I am talking to you about the party that gets most of its campaign funds from Wall Street and Big Business. I am talking about the party that gave us the phony Wall Street boom of the 1920's, and the Hoover depression that followed. I am talking to you about the party that gave us that no-account, do-nothing Republican Eightieth Congress.

The votes of the blue-collar workers, the blacks, and the farmers gave Truman his upset victory. But his was one of the last examples of a successful populist coalition.*

Something went out of liberalism after 1948. Its nature began to change, its goals diminished, its psychology became defensive, its character more middle class.

The reasons for this weakening of liberalism were complex.

---

* John Kennedy's 1960 victory combined the votes of minorities and the white working class, but the farm vote and much of the South was lost to him. Both the labor votes he did get and the rural votes he lost may have had as much to do with Catholicism as with his issueless campaign, which urged more defense spending to close the "missile gap" and the need "to get America moving again."

First, radicalism, which traditionally prods liberalism into its battles, collapsed in America. The persistent refusal of too many radical spokesmen—and liberal camp followers— to recognize the murderous truths about Stalin undercut much of radicalism's credibility. Too many purges and slave-labor camps had been excused or explained away as "historical inevitability" to justify listening to radical critiques of America. The growth of McCarthyism and the cold-war mentality took their toll: unions purged communists and radicals indiscriminately; the State Department became a citadel of conformity. The campuses, their intellectuals silenced and their students careerist, grew quiescent.

Faced with this challenge, men of good instincts but weak character went to excesses to prove their own anticommunism. Hubert Humphrey helped write the Communist Control Act of 1954; Dore Schary helped organize the Hollywood blacklist; *New York Post* editor James Wechsler attacked Joe McCarthy in his editorials—yet gave sixty names of communists to the FBI, which in turn gave them to McCarthy. The people who should have been thinking up new ideas, new programs, and new legislation—*the people claiming to represent the Left—were busy doing the work of the Right.*

In place of programs and issues, liberals became fixated by two Big Ideas, both of which were profoundly conservative.

One was the concept of "the end of ideology," crystallized by the Congress for Cultural Freedom (a CIA front) and popularized by Daniel Bell's book bearing that axiom as its title. The end of ideology was based on the presumption that all the large economic problems of America had already been solved; all that was now required were small adjustments, some minor technological tinkering with the soft machine at the top.

The foolishness of this notion has been proven many times over by the mass movements of the last ten years. But the injustices that animate these movements today were all present in the 1950's: poverty concealed by affluence, despoilation of the environment, powerlessness, the oppression of women, the spreading power of the military and the corporations, the decay of our cities, and, most clearly, racism. The intellectuals simply did not care to notice.

Bell's influential book was published in 1960, five years after Martin Luther King's bus boycott in Montgomery ignited the modern civil rights movement. Yet, in Bell's bulky index, there are only four references to Negroes, the longest dealing with crime statistics and none with the civil rights movement.

"The end of ideology" now appears to have been merely the very personal epitaph for one generation of intellectuals who had lost the capacity to imagine new radical movements growing within affluent America.

Bell's colleague, Seymour Martin Lipset, wrote, in the concluding chapter of his book, *Political Man,* which was published in 1959: "the fundamental political problems of the industrial revolution have been solved. . . . This very triumph of the democratic social revolution in the West ends domestic politics for those intellectuals who must have ideologies or Utopias to motivate them to political action."

What is astonishing is not that Lipset could have been so wrong, or so cocky, but that his view stood as the conventional wisdom among intellectuals for so long.

The second Big Idea that dominated liberal thinking in the 1950's was that the old economic passions of the 1930's had become outdated and the next great question modern reformers should take up was "the quality of life."

This notion revealed an immense white middle-class bias. It failed to look beneath the surface of a transient prosperity, as Michael Harrington would do in *The Other America,* published late in 1962. It also helped confuse sociology with economics, and culture with politics. Thus, the books middle-class liberals wrote and bought during the late 1950's were primarily studies of affluence and leisure: *The Lonely Crowd;*

The Affluent Society; *The Organization Man*; and *The Status Seekers*. Those writers who did insist on looking beneath the surface, who saw working-class injustices and who challenged the allocation of power—writers like Harvey Swados and C. Wright Mills—were not in fashion.

As late as 1960, Arthur Schlesinger, Jr. could write:

> This point—the quality of life—suggests the great difference between the politics of the '60s and the politics of the '30s. . . . The '60s will confront an economy of abundance. There are still pools of poverty which have to be mopped up; but the central problem will be increasingly that of fighting for individual dignity, identity, and fulfillment in an affluent mass society. . . . These issues will determine the quality of civilization to which our nation aspires in an age of ever increasing wealth and leisure.*

The notion that poverty was some minor puddle left over from the '30's, and could be "mopped up," now appears absurdly optimistic.

Something else, something not immediately apparent, began to happen after 1950. The Democratic party, the traditional party of reform, began to move away from the working masses, began to take on an elitist approach. Nationally, the divergence showed up in the 1950's in the characteristics of the two leading contenders for the party's presidential nomination.

On issues such as nuclear testing and civil liberties, Adlai Stevenson conducted himself better than most public men of his time. He was an attractive human being of taste and decency. His campaign speeches, although lacking in gut

---

* Among the ten issues of personal fulfillment listed by Schlesinger in the same article: "The prosecution of our weapons effort."

appeal, danced with wit and elegant phrases. Stevenson was a fine Tory.

But beginning with Stevenson's first campaign for the presidency, the Democratic party began to abandon its traditional role of representing the needs of the workers. Part of the problem was style: Stevenson conveyed the impression he did not really like people or politics. And part of the problem was programmatic: one reads Stevenson's old speeches in vain looking for a passion for raising the minimum wage, for inaugurating national health insurance, for taxing the rich, attacking corporate price fixing, or opening up the political process. Stevenson preferred to lecture sweaty crowds of workers about abstractions of foreign policy.

In 1954, in an attempt to deflate the Stevenson cult then so powerful among his fellow intellectuals, Irving Howe wrote in *Dissent*:

> Stevenson was the first of the liberal candidates in the post-Wilson era who made no effort to align himself with the plebian tradition or plebian sentiments. . . .
>
> Just as Stevenson bewitched the intellectuals by miming from on high their political impulses, so did he fail to attract very much enthusiasm among the workers. By and large they voted for him, but with little of the fervor they felt for Roosevelt and Truman. . . . Truman was one of the plebes, and after his triumph over Dewey, there was a remarkable elation in the Detroit auto plants. . . . A striking characteristic of Stevenson's campaign, as distinct from Roosevelt's or Truman's, was that he did not speak in the name of the poor or the workers. . . . The conservative press was always delighted to praise him for not indulging in Truman's "demagogy," that is, for not employing Truman's "anti-plutocrat" vocabulary.

The intellectuals, impoverished in their perceptions of domestic issues and—out of fear or complacency—accepting established views of foreign policy, loved Stevenson as much (if not more) for his style as for his restricted themes. And because of their literary perception of politics, intellectuals failed to recognize that Stevenson's great rival—Senator Estes Kefauver—was actually much more radical in his politics. (Perhaps if they had recognized this they would have been even cooler toward him, for the intellectuals of the 1950's were far from radical themselves.)

Kefauver was the other, older, and more traditional side of the Democratic party. He seemed to lack Stevenson's vague tragic quality, his urbane cultivation. But Kefauver's real sin was that, unlike the intellectuals, *he really liked politics.* And he knew how ordinary people lived.

Kefauver stood in the tradition of the best of southern populism. His whole public career bears witness to this. In September of 1946, while still a congressman, Kefauver began holding public hearings "to reverse the trend towards economic concentration of wealth." He never turned away from that theme. In 1947, Kefauver introduced legislation aimed at plugging a loophole in the Clayton Antitrust Act that had permitted one company to acquire the assets of a competing firm without actually merging (and thereby coming under Justice Department scrutiny) with it. In May of 1948, Kefauver wrote, in the *American Economic Review,* urging "new legislation to furnish the basis of prosecution of industrial giants." In 1950, as a freshman senator, Kefauver's landmark antitrust bill was enacted into law. A year later, he got $500,000 added to the budget of Justice's antitrust division. And it was Kefauver who, in the early years of the Eisenhower presidency, led the successful fight to prevent "the private power crowd" from taking over TVA. The act with which the public most readily associates Kefauver was his exposure of organized crime as a major political power in the big cities; and here too he was following populist tradition, for the hearings were the outgrowth of his concern over the corruption of the political process by men who hold vast and illegal wealth.

Even after his chances for the presidency were lost, Kefauver's passion for reform continued. He never settled for membership in the Senate's inner circle—the Club—but, instead, went on to conduct what may well have been the most important work of his career. Beginning in 1957, Kefauver initiated a series of hearings into price-fixing that ultimately exposed the steel, auto, and drug industries and that actually forced the big pharmaceutical companies to lower the prices of prescription drugs for the sick and the aged. The Kefauver hearings revealed more than price-fixing. They showed the full extent of economic concentration in the three industries investigated, and they provided the raw information on which the Justice Department—had it so chosen—could have moved against some of America's mightiest corporations.

Before his premature death, Kefauver was to move Congress to tighten loopholes in the Pure Food and Drug laws; there can be no doubt that, had he lived, he would have continued the landmark work he initiated as chairman of the Senate Subcommittee on Antitrust and Monopoly. His book *In a Few Hands: Monopoly Power in America* stands as a monument of economic fact-finding. He was, in David Bazelon's words, "the smartest Bryan ever." *

In 1952, Kefauver won thirteen of the nation's fourteen presidential primaries, but the Democratic convention, whose big-city bosses feared Kefauver's attacks on political and economic corruption, denied him either of the two top spots. Instead, they nominated Stevenson for president and John Sparkman of Alabama for vice president.

In 1968, the same two strands within liberalism—elitism and populism—were to clash once again in the party's presi-

---

* Kefauver was also more forthright on civil liberties than many of his Democratic colleagues. When the Communist Control Act, which outlawed the Communist party, was passed by the Senate in 1954, his was the only vote cast against the bill. In 1950, he was one of seven Senators who voted against the Internal Security (McCarran) Act.

dential primaries. Only the names changed. This time, the
battle was to be fought between Eugene McCarthy and
Robert Kennedy.

Eugene McCarthy was the hero of most of the college students and most of the intellectuals. Like Stevenson, McCarthy
possessed an intellectual's sensibility, and he hated the small,
cheap rituals of politics. McCarthy also earned—and deserved
—immense respect and support for his courage in challenging
Lyndon Johnson on the issue of the war in Vietnam. But
McCarthy, at bottom, was a snob who could twice tell his
upper- and middle-class university supporters in Oregon:

> I want you to remember when you go to the polls, that the
> more educated, more intelligent people vote for me, and the
> less educated people vote for my opponent.

During the Indiana primary, McCarthy refused on principle
even to mention the issue of crime, thus mirroring the distorted views then fashionable among most intellectuals: discussion of crime was merely a cloak for racism; concern over
crime was neither valid nor relevant. Later, in Oregon, he
refused to join Kennedy in urging new gun control laws as a
way of reducing violent crimes. Many feel he won the pro-gun
state by that stand.

But if McCarthy's 1968 campaign revealed an elitism, a
distance from the concerns of the working classes, his voting
record in the Senate equally demonstrates a strong streak of
antipopulism. In 1963, he voted to protect the oil depletion
allowance. In 1965, he voted against the amendment that
would have abolished the poll tax. While voting against tax
reform amendments, McCarthy recorded his vote in favor
of allowing corporate lobbyists to take their expenses as tax
deductions. And he authored the famous loophole amendment to the 1966 tax bill that permitted stockholders to
swap securities for shares in an investment fund without paying a capital gains tax. In 1969, McCarthy voted for Russell
Long—spokesman for the oil lobby—for Senate Whip rather

than for Edward Kennedy. Jeremy Larner, once a McCarthy speechwriter, assessed the Senator's politics this way in his fine book *Nobody Knows*:

> McCarthy was never for anything that challenged interests, rocked the boat, or threatened institutional reform. He was comfortable with the orderly process of Congress and its committee structure. . . . Given his willingness to balance interests rather than challenge them, it is hardly surprising that McCarthy was not a crusader when it came to consumer practices or tax reform.

In 1968, Robert Kennedy offered the Democratic party a second chance to stand with the people Dos Passos liked to call "the working stiffs." He was tough, and despite his wealth he had the capacity to see the world through the eyes of its victims—so he could communicate with the cop as well as the welfare mother. He hated crime as much as he hated war and he knew that the real victims of both were people without power. He could tell medical students what they didn't want to hear and force them to listen. He could tell collegians that their draft deferments put the risks of the war on the working whites and impoverished browns and blacks. And he could shout about tax reform in the town square of South Bend, and unite blacks, students, and factory workers in hope.

McCarthy's base was suburban, college educated: teachers, students, Republican businessmen, dovish housewives, managerial types. Workingmen and blacks sensed his indifference, sensed he had little interest in them or their problems, even if they didn't know his Senate voting record.

Kennedy, on the other hand, understood intuitively that the "less educated" were not necessarily the "less intelligent." He would not concede the factory workers of South Bend to George Wallace. And he would win 95 per cent of the ballots cast in Watts.

Kennedy's program and constituency in 1968 were, in embryo, the model for the future we are talking about in this book. McCarthy's model seems to us as narrow and as flawed as Hubert Humphrey's.

In 1948, the thread of populism was cut. Twice since then —first with Estes Kefauver and then with Robert Kennedy— an effort was made to pick up the severed tradition. Both times, the middle class, bewitched by style, failed the test.

Part Two ★ The Issues—and the Programs

*Ideas and issues are the glue that hold political coalitions to-
gether. What follows—the heart of our manifesto—are the
programs we think are most necessary to the creation of a
new populist majority—programs that unify on the basis of
class, rather than divide on the basis of race.*

*Some of these ideas, like tax reform and busting up cor-
porate monopolies, are traditional populist passions. Others,
like crime and the abuses of the labor unions, are usually
thought of as conservative. An idea like land redistribution
once dominated politics, but was not even mentioned in
either party platform in 1968.*

*For each issue we raise, we also offer specific programmatic
remedies. The following areas of concern certainly do not
exhaust the populist possibilities. They are merely our own
priorities, our effort to shift the liberal imagination away
from the faddish and the mechanistic, toward deeper but
"unsexy" problems like the conduct of banks and federal regulatory agencies and the dangerous concentration of ownership
of the mass media.*

*Our purpose is to make public issues out of private discon-
tents, so that new popular movements may take root and
grow.*

3 ★ Concentrated Economic Power

IMAGINE A country that exists within the United States. Its chief executive gets paid four times as much as the President of the United States. Its budget is bigger than those of the three biggest states and bigger than that of all but two nations in the world. Imagine that its enormous wealth has purchased the loyalty of congressmen, senators, and federal officials; and that its lobbyists can shape the tax laws, criminal laws, and economic policies of Washington. Suppose, too, that the United States found that this nation within a nation was directly responsible for the deaths of tens of thousands of citizens, and was responsible as well for a third of our air pollution.

If the American people ever were confronted with such a conspiracy, there would be national outrage. Declarations of war would be drafted. Very likely, federal troops would be sent across the border of this aggressor nation to stop the killing and poisoning of our citizens.

Such a nation does exist—today—within our borders. Its leaders are elected by only the wealthiest of people and institutions. It has stood accused of precisely these acts against the American people and it has stood mute, preferring to rely on its economic and political power to exempt it from the laws that apply to the rest of us.

The name of this state is General Motors.

In 1969, a government indictment accused its leaders of conspiring with their fellow auto-makers to block pollution controls on autos—controls that could have lessened GM's contribution to pollution, which by itself accounts for 35 per cent of the air pollutants in America's air. Using its enormous power, GM and its fellow companies got the Justice Department to sign a consent decree, thereby blocking any attempt at either public prosecution or private suits for damages. And, during the entire time that GM's hired hands in Washington were meeting in secret with the Justice Department, the public was completely excluded from any part in the decision about this corporate criminal activity.

General Motors, with its 50 per cent–plus share of the market, virtually controls industry decisions on styling, production, pricing, and automobile engineering. Yet, from the time fifty years ago when its president refused to introduce safety glass, to the mid-1960's when GM scorned collapsible steering columns, and on down to the present as the company continues to ignore the case against the internal combustion engine, GM has chosen the status quo (and exorbitant profits) over policies that would protect motorist and pedestrian alike.

If any individual had committed such acts and produced such consequences, he would have been pilloried, prosecuted, and condemned as socially pathological, if not subversive. But General Motors continues to profit from death, pollution, and inflation. And its leaders are given testimonials instead of subpoenas, and are on commissions and charity boards and in good-government associations.

That is what it means to possess massive economic power in America. And that kind of power is the defining characteristic of the American economy.

For many liberals, the fear of enormous private corporate power seems a relic of another time, a throwback to the superheated rhetoric of the trusts and Teddy Roosevelt's "malefactors of great wealth." Surely, with the New Deal, public controls on excessive private wealth were secured and settled.

But while liberalism was abandoning its roots in economic justice, private concentrated control of our economic system was increasing. In 1956, 16.6 per cent of all American profits went to seven companies; by 1964, those same seven companies—GM, Ford, AT&T, Standard Oil of New Jersey, Texaco, Gulf Oil, and IBM—earned 25 per cent of all American profits.

In 1950, the 100 largest corporations controlled 38.6 per cent of total industrial assets in the United States. By 1965, the 100 biggest corporations held control of 45.4 per cent. And the 200 biggest had hold of *two-thirds* of the wealth of manufacturing corporations, a greater share than the top 1,000 had held in 1941.

Bigness, wealth, and power have replaced initiative and opportunity as the key factors in determining who succeeds and who fails in America's economy. The image of the small, determined entrepreneur, doggedly competing against established giants and winning a place for his new idea, is just that—an image, suitable for chamber of commerce speeches and almost completely divorced from reality. Instead, a small group of businesses dominate the critical segments of American industry, and use that domination to keep profits high and competitors out. And we pay the price of that control.

Three of those seven supergiants that absorb a quarter of all domestic profits are oil companies: big businesses for whom the tax laws and foreign policies of America protect and insulate wealth. The wage-earner pays for the oil depletion, drilling, and other allowances that let these companies pay a lower rate of taxes than a policeman or a teacher. Oil import quotas cost Americans between $5–7 billion a year; and for a New Yorker, that means an extra $102 every year to drive his car and heat his home. Meanwhile, after-tax income of the major oil companies for the first half of 1971 was nearly $3 billion—more than 20 per cent of *all* industrial profits.

The 1971 Nader Task Force report on economic concentration—*The Closed Enterprise System*—detailed the ways in which monopoly power cost the people of America:

A worldwide quinine cartel fixes the drug's price, thereby causing the price to rise from 37 cents to $213 an ounce.

A conspiracy to fix the price of tetracycline forces the sick to pay $51 for 100 tablets; the conspiracy is broken—and the price plunges to $5 an ounce.

A price-fixing conspiracy drives the price for a half-gallon of milk 11 cents above the competitive rate. (Such milk conspiracies have been found in almost every big American city over the last twenty years.)

A $35 million conspiracy drives the price of a loaf of bread up 20 per cent in Seattle.

These are specific and illegal acts. But the greater cost, the greater outrage, is the entire pattern by which the economy is more and more taken out of the hands of individuals and placed under the control of corporate giants.

This economic domination is not confined to the 100 and 200 largest corporations. Banks, with massive power in the form of deposits to lend and invest, are gaining an ever stronger grip on America's economy. Forty-nine banks, which together control $135 billion in assets, have directors who also sit on 6,591 different—and sometimes competing—corporations. And of the $1 trillion in institutional investments, more than $700 billion is controlled by banks. Thus, the biggest of industry is in turn owned by the biggest of financial institutions.

And the big have been getting bigger. A little-noticed report in June, 1971 by the House Judiciary Committee's Antitrust Subcommittee concluded that, after eighty years of laws, declarations, and lawsuits designed to increase diversity in the marketplace, concentration had grown steadily.* The spread of giant firms gaining power *in different areas of economic life* was perhaps the most compelling kind of evidence. In 1958, 29 of the top 100 firms were among the four big powers in four or more industries; by 1963, 48 of the top 100 were among the top four in four or more different parts of the American economy. From 1929 to 1968—during a time of consistent national leadership by liberal-based economic concepts—the share of the top 200 corporations grew from 46.1 to more than 60 per cent of total manufacturing assets.

The impact of aggregate power—the spread of control from one into many parts of our economic life—can be seen in the oil industry, the most privileged and profitable private industry. Its enormous profits shielded by tax gimmicks, import quotas, and artificial restrictions on output, the oil industry is now moving to monopolize potentially competing fuels. According to 1970 figures, twenty of the biggest oil companies control 60 per cent of the country's natural gas production; twenty-nine of the top 50 coal companies, with about 30 per cent of total production, are now controlled by oil companies; so are 45 per cent of known oil reserves. And all of this control has been exercised without a move from the Antitrust Division of the Department of Justice, which is charged with the job of blocking monopolization in America.

Further, the huge merger wave of the 1960's brought thousands of once independent companies under the control of a relative handful of business giants. More than 4,500 mergers and acquisitions took place in 1969, affecting assets of more than $20 billion—an increase of 1000 per cent over 1960 and 80 per cent above the already accelerated 1967 rate.

---

* The committee's report drew a distinction between *market* concentration and aggregate concentration. Market concentration—the share of any one product or service area by big companies—had held steady, itself a sign of failure of public policy. But the share of the total economic pie held by the biggest of giants had sharply grown since the end of World War II.

Even large companies found themselves gobbled up by the bigger fish: in 1968, 205 firms with $10 million or more in assets were swallowed up by bigger brothers representing 10 per cent of all manufacturers in that size range. And while the stock market collapse of 1969–70 and the crash of many conglomerates brought an ebbing of the merger wave—a decline which Antitrust Chief Richard MacLaren said erased the need for new laws—the fact is that the gathering of economic power in a few hands increased. Even in the "morning-after" atmosphere of 1970, more than 2,000 companies were merged or absorbed—ten times as many as in 1950. And the slowing of merger-mania did not mean that concentration was reversed —only that it slowed and consolidated. The thousands of formerly independent firms, representing diverse and potentially competitive forces in our economic life, did not come back into being; they remained subordinated to the will of a few decision-makers.

In this sense, then, the decade of the 1960's brought us closer to the grim future prophesied in the 1969 Federal Trade Commission study: that of "a few hundred business suzerainties under whose influence a multitude of small, weak, quasi-independent corporations will be permitted a subsidiary and supplemental role." Whatever name we give to that rapidly approaching system—the corporate state or *1984* —it is not a competitive, open economy.

The fact of concentration is indisputable. The more crucial question, however, is the *consequence* of concentration—what it means to the average American. It is here that the full impact of a corporate America—with wealth enriching wealth at our cost—can be understood. For it is not just the economic sense of fairness that suffers at the hands of huge private power. "In addition to serious economic consequences," the 1971 House Antitrust Subcommittee study said, "increases in aggregate concentration jeopardize social and political goals." Put briefly, many of our most cherished—and hopeful—ideas about how a free society ought to operate are crushed by the growth of concentrated economic power. Its consequences, then, are worth examining step-by-step.

First, bigness means *higher profits*. A White House economic report in 1969 disclosed that businesses in highly concentrated industries* made 50 per cent higher profits than businesses in unconcentrated industries. In the last ten years, America's giant corporations—those with $1 billion or more in assets—have substantially increased their share of net assets (from 26 to 46 per cent) and of profits (from 36 to 50 per cent). Today, the biggest 1 per cent of America's corporations control 86 per cent of the assets and 88 per cent of the net profits of all manufacturing corporations. The gap between the big boys and the rest is so enormous that the 87 biggest businesses netted as much in 1969 as 649,000 smaller ones. By contrast, the smaller companies—those with $10 million or less in assets—hold 14 per cent of manufacturing assets, compared with 20 per cent at the start of the decade.† In other words, as far as profits in the American economy are concerned, the race is not to the swift, but to the huge.

Second, bigness means *immunity from the rules of a competitive economy*. As Senator Kefauver's hearings in the late 1950's disclosed, industries in which a few giants hold sway —such as auto and steel—don't respond to the traditional laws of supply and demand. They are powerful enough to choose a predetermined profit—20 per cent a year in the

---

* An industry in which four firms or less account for 70 per cent of sales is highly concentrated—or, in the poetic term of economists, "oligopolistic."

† In fairness, we should note that one study—released in November of 1970 by the UCLA Graduate School of Business—argued that "there is no significant relationship between the concentration of an industry, and the profit rates of companies in the industry." Also in fairness, we note that the study was financed by General Motors, United States Steel, AT&T, IT&T, Alcoa, and Litton Industries.

case of General Motors—and set prices to meet that profit regardless of the demand for autos, and regardless of how tough it is for the rest of us to keep our heads above water.

Thus, in January of 1958, in the midst of the second Eisenhower recession, the *New York Times* reported that "more industries than ever before are in a position to 'administer' their prices—hold them high in the face of sluggish demand. For example, current steel prices at the mills have not fallen despite a slump in demand that has brought operations down from nearly 100 per cent of capacity to about 60 per cent." Later that year, the steel companies confirmed this judgment by actually *raising* prices $4.50 a ton.

Nor were the steel companies alone. During the recessions of the 1950's, every unconcentrated industry sampled in one study followed the normal pattern when demand drops— they lowered prices. But 13 of 16 concentrated industries raised their prices. The impact of this kind of immunity is enormous. Firms as basic to our economy as steel are able to maintain exorbitant profits by jacking up prices even as joblessness is growing by hundreds of thousands. The theoretical "competitors" automatically follow the pricing lead of the giants and that means that price increases in the cost of basic necessities are hitting the wage-earner and the poor just as their struggle for economic survival is worsening.*

The ability of big business to shield high profits from the impact of hard times suggests another, rarely examined consequence of concentration: *inflation*. Usually, the debate between conservative and liberal economists over the loss of purchasing power and the squeeze on the family budget focuses on wages, prices, and interest rates. But there is evidence

---

* So, in 1956, Ford made the mistake of releasing its 1957 price list two weeks before GM. Ford showed a 2.9 per cent average increase. One week after GM released its list—with a whopping 6.1 per cent increase for Chevrolet—Ford issued upwardly revised prices. As for steel, in *U.S. v Bethlehem Steel Corporation*, the government stated that U.S. Steel "initiates the price changes for steel products and that its lead is followed by all other steel producers."

that the enormous profits racked up by corporate concentration—profits linked not to efficiency or product superiority, but to lack of competition—are themselves a hidden contributor to inflation. One economist has concluded that the rate of near-monopoly profits—close to 15 per cent a year—*by itself* adds 3 per cent to the annual rate of inflation. But more significant, we believe, is *where this profit goes.* It is indisputable—for all of the Nixon–Rotary Club–Young Republican nonsense about people's capitalism and the millions of orphans, widows, and wounded war veterans living off a share of America's profits—that *corporate profits go to stockholders and America's stockholders are the rich. About 1.6 per cent of America's adult population owns 82.4 per cent of the publicly held shares in the nation's corporations.* It is this tiny minority of shareholding Americans that gather in the superprofits generated by the power of big business to stifle competition and manipulate prices without fear of challenge. When we recognize that officers of these superbusinesses often collect more money from their stockholdings and stock-option privileges than from their huge salaries, we can see where much of our money goes: not to the community at large, not to wage-earners, not into more efficient products, but into the bank accounts, trust funds, and holdings of the richest 1.6 per cent of Americans.

Further, the structure and position of these near-monopoly businesses offer an open invitation to sloth and waste. We recognize the legitimate fear of many conservatives that government bureaucracies, with no responsibilities to be efficient and productive, can often spend a great deal of money doing nothing; we recognize, too, that when labor unions win wage increases far higher than their work productivity earns, inflation is inevitable. And many conservatives now admit that the Defense Department has been a major source of waste —$5 billion spent for a $2 billion plane that couldn't fly, 50 cent screws bought for $25, and $20 billion spent on missile systems that never worked—with all the extra costs passed on to the taxpayer. Regulated industries, like electric utilities and telephone companies, are often top-heavy with waste because their profits are guaranteed by law and there is neither effective competition nor effective regulation to promote efficiency.

What is now becoming clear is that *exactly the same thing is true of industries in which corporate and financial near-monopolies escape competition.* In effect, concentrated industries are made up of firms that control their own profits without either government regulation or market competition. And thus we have the spectacle of modern baronies, complete with $20 billion worth of expense accounts, corporate compensation running into the $800,000-a-year range, a fleet of corporate jets, sixty-story skyscrapers made of marble, and the kind of profligacy that a company can engage in when it knows that there is no possible challenge to its economic might. That kind of profligacy is a key element of the inflationary spiral.

The defenders of the "corporation state" argue that bigness is essential to progress. The evidence proves very much the opposite. Big companies have tremendous investments in the status quo; any new way of doing things threatens enormous costs at best and is, at worst, a challenge to their economic might. For instance, an automobile that runs on steam, or electricity, or something other than the internal combustion engine, threatens huge retooling costs for giants like GM and Ford—but it also threatens the gas and oil industry, which sells 60 billion gallons of gasoline every year to motorists. Kefauver's hearings showed how, time and again, major innovations in engineering and technology—for example, the automatic gear shift and the puncture-proof tire—were kept out of production long after they had been developed and found practical. In each case, retooling costs or the sales impact on related industries entered into the decision to shelve production.

Virtually every new technique in steel production—techniques that made it safer, quicker, and cheaper to produce steel—was rejected by U.S. Steel, Bethlehem, and the other industry giants because they had enormous capital investments in the outmoded blast furnaces in Pittsburgh. It took foreign mills to show how it could be done. And studies of new inventions—from the Xerox copying machine to computers, from transistors to the Polaroid camera—have shown that individuals, not corporations, developed them, and then had to fight the established giants every step of the way. (Often, big companies like General Electric and Westinghouse have used their economic power to buy out small potential competitors, and then market the inventions they themselves had been unable to perfect. And it has not been uncommon that patents have been bought by large companies intent on ensuring that they never be developed.)

There is, too, another cost of concentrated power. It is a cost that cannot be measured by economists or accountants, but it is, perhaps, more intolerable than all of the others. It is the cost that Louis Brandeis a half century ago called "the curse of bigness." Of all the lost causes fought for the preservation of the American promise, none is more painful—and less remembered—than the campaign at the outset of the twentieth century to break up the oversized economic giants that were strangling independent businessmen and subjugating suppliers, customers, and workers alike to the whims of the robber barons. Brandeis and a handful of Progressives recognized the inevitable consequences of giantism in the marketplace. Big business, they said, would breed big labor, and then big government to mediate disputes between these forces: then, slowly but surely, we would witness the disappearance of the individual citizen's sense that he counts for something; that what he thinks or says or does makes any difference. Today, after six decades of following the course warned against by Brandeis, we find ourselves surrounded by giant institutions on every side of our lives, while politicians debate which of these giants shall have a greater or lesser role in running our lives—but never whether these institutions ought to possess such power. And names become numbers whether we confront GM, or the AFL-CIO, or the FTC, or NYU—and that essential quality of democracy, the sense of debate and struggle and accommodation among people who meet face to face, is true of almost no part of our lives.

We are not Luddites; we do not propose to smash the machines and turn America into an agrarian society. You do not run America's economy from the corner grocery store. But the constant yearning of Americans—of all ages, races, and classes—for a sense that *some* part of our lives be closer to human scale must be counted when figuring the enormous cost of concentrated power.

There is, further, the pattern of countervailing concentrations of power to act like the financial elite—protecting their small shares of power out of the conviction that the "fix," the special privilege, is the only way that security can be found. We find this all across our society:

Unions close their rolls to all but the relatives of members, and demand wasteful featherbedding rules to assure their continued employment.

Teachers fight "voucher" plans to give the children of low- and moderate-income families an alternative to compulsory public school education.

State universities oppose college financing to enable financially strapped students to go to whatever college accepts them, rather than forcing them into state schools for lack of funds.

Doctors demand "professionalism" to keep the supply of doctors low and their origins middle- and upper-class.

College students who proclaim their concern for "justice" support student deferments that protect their safety while putting the burden of war on low-income whites, browns, and blacks.

Suburban liberals sing "We Shall Overcome" and send checks south, while urging acreage and zoning restrictions to enable only the most affluent Americans to move into their neighborhoods.

All of these positions represent a defense of privilege; *all* are unjust; and *none* begin to match the scope and cost of privilege and profit exacted from us by the wealthy.* The elite has taught us well; and so today, many of the most emotional of disputes among natural political allies stem from a dispute over the scraps of privilege—and from the conviction that special treatment is the only way we can make it in America.

Beyond what we pay in dollars and what we lose in new ideas, monopoly power has become a kind of private government, often exercising greater power than the elected public officials of the United States—including the president.

If the steel companies of Indiana and Ohio decide they will use rivers as open sewers, the rivers die. No local government can compete with the sheer economic clout of a U.S. Steel in Gary. It controls by itself too many jobs and too many lives to be bucked successfully (or even to be taxed like other businesses; U.S. Steel each year tells Gary how much it intends to contribute in lieu of local taxes). If petrochemical companies in New Jersey pour filth into Raritan Bay and choking fumes into the air over Elizabeth, Perth Amboy, and Staten Island, who is to stop them? When a giant coal company decides it will strip mine because strip mining cuts costs

---

* Organized labor is a powerful economic counterweight to corporate power; some unions, notably in the construction field, have the capacity to administer wages without regard to competitive reality, in much the same way giant businesses can adjust prices free from the pressures of the laws of supply and demand. But the idea that unions as such have the same measure of economic power as their corporate employers is absurd. Look, for example, at the fifty-nine day United Auto Workers strike against General Motors. The UAW is one of the largest, best organized unions in the nation. Its strike hit GM with a $77 million loss for the third quarter. But the loss was temporary. General Motors finished the year with a $609 million profit. By contrast, the UAW completely exhausted its strike fund, and was forced to mortgage its headquarters in order to survive. GM still owns its offices and factories.

and increases profits, it does it; no Appalachian government, no Congress, has yet been able to determine that preserving land has a higher value than making profits. If auto companies want to make auto transportation the dominant mode of movement in America—and in one ugly package, scar the face of the country, wipe out stable working-class neighborhoods in the cities (and replace them with highway ramps), add to congestion and the pollution of our air, and divert attention from alternative mass transit forms—it is done. The U.S. Government, in the form of a $60 billion Highway Trust Fund, subsidizes General Motors, Ford, *et al.,* while $80-a-week factory employees pay 30 or 50 cents to ride a filthy, dangerous, debilitating mass transit system.

In this sense, the private nation within a nation does exist. It is not, for the most part, conspiratorial. It does not control every lever of every government. But, like any institution, monopoly power protects itself from attack. It is willing to enter the political process, to threaten elected officials, to bribe politicians in the form of lavish campaign contributions, to make the laws, rules, and processes of government responsive not to people, but to the handful of the richest Americans who control the big business of America.

The kind of power that monopoly interests hold is often technical, undramatic, mechanical. It is not proclaimed in speeches; instead, it is negotiated in court cases, which reporters often don't bother to cover; it is insulated in the technicalities of the Tax Code, or in obscure pieces of legislation that turn out to be critical—and disastrous—for the public interest.

The only way monopoly power will be curtailed is if a political movement recognizes its reality and its dangers. Until we learn that laws can kill; that court settlements can perpetuate injustice; and that regulations can mean life and death to us, we will continue to cheer for promises of political justice —while in the closed corners of America, the men who serve monopoly power win the real battles every time.

To combat this kind of concentration does not require major new legislation. It requires, instead, the use of existing antitrust legislation to put into effect what those laws intended all along: to combat concentration, break up private corporations whose power has grown dangerous, protect smaller, less powerful entrepreneurs, and secure a diversity of independent managers and owners. Despite the predominance of economists in the antitrust debates, these laws were never intended solely as economic tools. They were based in major part on the belief that huge pockets of private economic power were suspect at best and dangerous at worst. Whether it is an economic giant buying a locally owned business and removing decisions from that locality, or a merger that results in the loss of a trusted decision-maker who once ran an independent concern, the social costs of economic concentration are critical and real—and so too is the direct economic cost to average Americans of economic concentration.

We advocate these kinds of countermeasures:

ONE   Break up the biggest corporations

There is no reason why General Motors, which makes five different lines of cars, buses, and trucks, as well as electrical appliances, should be under one roof. Despite the frantic efforts of GM's management to combine its operations so as to thwart any future moves against itself, the divisions of GM could be separated and sold to new owners with minimal inconvenience. The same is true of U.S. Steel, which as several economists have noted, is nothing more than an aggregation of dozens of independently functioning steel mills spread around the country. If the Attorney General's office can prove the charges of exorbitant profiteering and technologically inefficient and dangerous methods, the courts should order "divestiture." It is a well-established legal step to promoting competition; it was, in fact, proposed by the President's Council of Economic Advisers in 1969. And companies like GM have clearly earned that step.

TWO   Ban all mergers and corporate take-overs by the top 200 corporations

While the debate about concentration rages, the fact of concentration continues. In 1968, mergers increased 67 per cent over 1967's rate, and the 1969 figures went up another 16 per cent. Only with the conglomerate disasters of 1969 and 1970 did the trend slow down.

In the single year of 1968, 10 per cent of all independent manufacturers in the $10 million-plus-class were absorbed by even bigger giants. In the face of this, the government could, at the least, order a two- or three-year "cooling off" period while the social and political costs of mergers were seriously debated. (House Judiciary Committee Chairman Emanuel Celler has already suggested that none of the top 500 corporations be allowed to acquire any corporation with assets of more than $100,000.) We have had a wage freeze and a price freeze; a "merger freeze" would at least give us time to think before concentration further destroyed what is left of a competitive economy.

THREE   Put persistent antitrust violators in jail

We do not believe that criminals of any kind should escape the force of the law. But in this country, criminals who wear a suit and tie are not considered lawbreakers. They may cheat the public out of millions of dollars; they may keep vital foods and drugs from the poor, fix prices in violation of the law, make decisions that kill untold numbers of people: but if they are clean-shaven and well-groomed and hold a corporate title, they are respected businessmen. Apart from the electrical companies brought up on price-fixing charges in the early 1960's when Robert Kennedy was Attorney General, few of the big boys have ever gone to jail and few of their companies have ever been brought into court to determine reparations. But an antitrust policy that said flatly, "a rich criminal is still a criminal" might well impose a deterrent in the minds of other businessmen, whose reputations are far more fragile than a ghetto youngster's.

FOUR Change the tax laws and accounting tools that make mergers among the big corporations desirable

Today, many firms merge not because it is efficient, but because the tax laws permit wealthy corporations to shelter profits in the financial structure of the acquired firm. Further, the techniques of accountants can make a firm look more profitable than it really is when it takes over a smaller, well-run business. A drastic change in these laws and rules would forestall and quite possibly prevent many mergers.

FIVE Ensure that the corporation that has broken the law suffers the penalty

If the prospect of jail may deter the businessman from engaging in illegal practices, the prospect of stiff financial penalties may have the same effect on corporate management. At the very least, the government must cooperate with private and local suits for damages that are the outgrowth of federal cases. More important, given the extensive amount of government contract work that is handled by the largest corporations, stipulations should be drawn up forbidding—for a period of time—future contracts with companies proven to have engaged in illegal actions. If in fact such a company is the only one capable of fulfilling a government contract, antitrust investigations ought to be pursued. It is even possible that our patent laws will need to be overhauled in those instances where control has led to abuse of the public interest.

4 ★ The Money Changers: Banking and Insurance

In 1932, with America's financial institutions at the brink of collapse, Franklin D. Roosevelt told America in his inaugural address that "the money changers have fled from their high seats in the temple."

The money changers are running the temple now; using their enormous, largely unseen economic power to enrich the rich and impoverish the poor, destroy neighborhoods, and protect economic privilege.

The economic manipulations and the special treatment of commercial banks and insurance companies—the two key groups of money managers—are mostly ignored by the press; politicians, with rare exceptions like Congressman Wright Patman, leave them alone or actively cooperate with them. Nobody holds protest rallies about the over-all economic practices of banks—only their investments in the war and in racist nations like South Africa and Rhodesia have been publicized and drawn opposition.

But banks and insurance companies are among the most

important forces behind the unfair distribution of wealth and power in America. Protected by federal law, given dozens of special breaks on their taxes, permitted to build degrees of concentrated economic power long outlawed in other areas of economic life, banks and insurance companies have used this power deliberately and systematically to redistribute wealth and power away from the poor and working people, toward the rich.

First, some raw facts of economic life. Banks control more money than the United States Government; and that control is concentrated among a handful of the big boys. At the end of 1969, banks controlled trust accounts which alone were worth $280 billion—about $50 billion more than the total U.S. Government operating budget. (The total assets held by commercial banks exceeded $700 billion in 1970.) This trust money was spread over 3,100 commercial banks. But 19 big banks controlled more than half of that money. The life insurance companies controlled about $190 billion. But it is virtually a fiction to separate these figures out. For, while the law says banks and insurance companies are supposed to compete with each other for investments, the facts are that they work together as a giant economic combine.

We can measure the concentrated economic power another way—by looking at just the ten biggest banks and the ten biggest insurance companies. The ten largest commercial banks had, at the end of 1970, $130 billion in deposits—about a fourth of the deposits of *all* the commercial banks in the United States. They controlled $150 billion in assets. And the ten biggest life insurance companies controlled $130 billion in assets—or more than half of the assets of all the life insurance companies in America.

The huge monies controlled by banks and insurance companies come from several sources: deposits of average working Americans, estates of the wealthy that banks manage, insurance premiums, pension funds of labor and management that banks and insurance companies invest. This money, more than any kind of government policy, controls the American economy: because only the money changers have the capital to lend for starting up new businesses, helping troubled companies, and building housing. Thus, the decisions of banks and insurance companies determine which neighborhoods are renewed and which decay; which businesses can expand and which cannot; what kind of housing is built for what kind of family. This enormous capital is, in the phrase of Louis Brandeis, "other people's money," but it is effectively under the control of the financial institutions; the people who earn it in the first place have no say about how it is to be used.

It becomes critical, then, to know who makes decisions about what banks and insurance companies do. We elect the legislatures, the congressmen, the mayors, governors, and presidents who we think are setting national policies. But when it comes to the basic gut question of who shares the benefits of the enormous monies now in the hands of banks and insurance companies, the answer is that the overwhelming majority of Americans have no voice at all. The decisions are made by a tiny minority of even the wealthiest citizens, who dominate the decision-making boards of the money changers.

The key device in the world of high finance is the *interlocking directorate*—a device outlawed for most of the economic world by the antitrust laws of a half-century ago. In essence, the interlocking directorate is a tool to keep economic power in a few hands by naming the same people to the boards of directors of most of the big companies. It is outlawed among industrial competitors: a director of General Motors cannot also be a director of Ford or Chrysler. It is outlawed among buyers and sellers: if U.S. Steel does business with GM, it would be dangerous to have the same people in charge of both companies.

But, thanks to a loophole in the antitrust laws, such multiple directorships are not outlawed for banks and insurance companies. The result is that money managers each control each other; and the boards of directors of the big banks serve as meeting grounds for companies that are supposed to be competing with each other.

For example, the ten biggest life insurance companies have thirty interlocks with the ten biggest commercial banks. Nine of the same men who govern the Mutual Life Insurance Company also sit on the boards of six of the ten big banks. And this pattern also infests the top ranks of the banking profession: Chemical Bank of New York interlocks with twelve other commercial banks—"competitors" in theory—four savings institutions, thirteen insurance companies, and six other money changers; First National City Bank, with more than $20 billion in deposits alone, interlocks with six other banks and twenty-one insurance companies; Chase Manhattan, the Rockefeller-controlled bank with more than $23 billion in deposits, interlocks with six other commercial banks and six insurance companies.

Perhaps most stunning is the way banks bring competitors together on their boards of directors. On its own board, *Chase Manhattan* has directors from competing companies in the three vital industries—steel, automobiles, and oil. Thus, Chase directors are also directors of U.S. Steel, American Smelting and Refining, Allegheny Ludlum Steel, Pioneer Aluminum, and Titanium Metal; of General Motors and Chrysler; and of Atlantic Richfield, Standard Oil of New Jersey, and Standard Oil of Indiana. *Morgan Guaranty Trust* brings together directors of Atlantic Richfield, Continental Oil, and Standard Oil of New Jersey; of U.S. Steel and Bethlehem; and of General Motors and Ford. *Continental Illinois National Bank and Trust* has on its board directors of Standard Oil of Indiana, Universal Oil, Pure Oil, and Union Oil; and of Sears Roebuck and Montgomery Ward.

A 1969 Federal Trade Commission staff study revealed that 49 major banks in ten cities held 786 interlocking directorates with 236 of the nation's top 500 corporations; 146 interlocks with 29 of the 50 biggest insurance companies; and 86 interlocks with 22 of the 50 biggest utilities. In 176 cases, these huge banks held 5 per cent or more of the common stock of the 500 biggest corporations. That is financial concentration on an enormous scale.

The usual defense made in response to an attack on these kinds of interlocking directorates is that no one should presume that the men (women have virtually no place on these boards) who run these institutions are dishonest. But that is not the point. Professor Edward Herman of the Wharton School of Finance has put the dilemma this way:

> Directors are not likely to be scoundrels, they are likely to be gentlemen. And gentlemen respect other gentlemen with whom they are closely associated. And that is far more profound a problem than scoundrelism. The problem is that if gentlemen associate on boards, they are not likely to do something really hostile to the interests of the other gentlemen with whom they are associated.

The danger of this kind of narrowly held economic power can be shown by a hypothetical example and proved by real ones. Suppose, for example, an inventor came up with a new kind of car that ran on steam or efficient electricity; suppose further that the car was made with a nonsteel alloy. Suppose he then went to Morgan Guaranty Trust for a loan to get started. In banking, the ultimate decision on who gets big loans is made by the board of directors. What chance is there that directors from GM, Ford, U.S. Steel, Bethlehem, and the three giant oil companies would agree to finance a venture that would threaten the profits of *all* of those companies? There wouldn't have to be a conspiracy; a simple judgment based on prudent business practice and the worldview of these directors would be enough.

Real examples of the dangers of interlocking directorates are pervasive. They are as basic as the small savings and loan association in Missouri whose board of directors includes many with an interest in a local lumber yard. According to one Missouri congressman, applicants for home loans have been "persuaded" to purchase their lumber from that particular yard; those who refuse have found loans impossible to get. Such examples are magnified in scope and in impact when they concern the larger banks. The Bank of America with assets of $29 billion—the largest in the nation—sold savings bank life insurance to customers and used Prudential as its agent. The cost to the buyer was 39 cents for each $100 of insurance. Prudential, which had interlocking directors with the Bank, in turn gave a part of the proceeds to the Bank of America. Thus, the higher the insurance costs to customers, the more the Bank would make, and, in 1965, the Bank of America pressured Prudential to raise its price to 61 cents for each $100 of insurance. The result was more than $1.2 million in proceeds to the Bank of America. Here again, the economic ties between the money changers produced profit for both of them and higher costs for the average American. Had representatives of labor, blacks, or consumers been on either board of directors, such a move could not have been made without enormous objections. But because the economic elite is isolated in its management of money, the result was profit for the wealthy and victimization for the consumer.

One of the most astonishing facts of the banking and life insurance businesses is that they are "recession proof." People, frightened about the economy, tend to save more, and this means more money on deposit for banks to invest. Meanwhile, the Federal Reserve System, which is controlled by a narrow financial elite, makes sure that interest rates go high enough to protect bank profits.*

* Congressman Patman, chairman of the House Banking and Currency Committee, who has waged a virtual one-man fight against the economic power of banks, detailed how commercial banks dominate the process for selecting members of the Federal Reserve System in a

According to *Fortune* magazine's figures for 1970, commercial banks increased their assets 11.5 per cent, deposits 12.1 per cent, and stockholders' equity 7.8 per cent. The per-share performance of banks showed an 11.7 per cent gain. What these figures mean is that during the depths of a recession, commercial banks—just the fifty biggest—hauled in $1.76 billion of net income.

The life insurance companies were equally impressive. The fifty biggest added $76.6 billion to their insurance in force, for a total of more than *$1 trillion*. The gains in premium and annuity income grew by $25 billion, for the biggest gain since at least the mid-sixties; not bad for a recession year.

It would be at least defensible if these enormous profits were the result of business acumen or new breakthroughs in management and service. But the real source of such profits is linked directly to the government. Federal laws and policies are designed to keep profits in the hands of stockholders— *not* in the accounts of depositors. The most obvious of these laws is the Banking Act of 1933 (and, as amended, 1935) that prohibits paying interest on checking accounts. This law means that every American with a checking account is making an interest-free loan to a bank; which can then turn around, invest the money in loans, and earn the interest on it for itself. As an example, if a commercial bank has $50 million in checking accounts, and invests just 10 per cent of that amount over a year, it will earn $300,000 in interest. The depositors will earn nothing. Instead, they will be charged 10 to 15 cents every time they write a check, plus a service charge.

But the most important government regulations that help banks and insurance companies pile up profits are the tax

---

1970 speech. The upshot is that the men who control interest rates are chosen by committees that are in fact controlled by commercial bankers. Their selections to the Federal Open Market Committee— the quasi-public body that sets fiscal policy—meet in secret. But the banking establishment knows its own interests are always foremost.

laws. Again, we are dealing with highly technical regulations that most people simply do not understand. But the result is that *banks and insurance companies pay far lower taxes than other private enterprises, and lower taxes than most middle-class and skilled blue-collar workers.*

Banks, for example, can deduct "bad debt" reserves that are six times higher than their "real" debts. This law was written to protect the economy against the kind of bank runs that occurred in the 1930's But its current effect is to let banks amass profits in an untaxed, constantly growing pile. The 1969 Tax Reform Act changes this for some banks, but its full effect won't be felt until 1988. Meanwhile, the Treasury is depleted by hundreds of millions of dollars every year.

Banks are also heavy investors in state and local tax-free bonds; they own more than $50 billion of the $115 billion in tax-free government bonds. But the interest they pay to depositors whose savings they "borrow" to buy these bonds is fully tax deductible; in essence, the government subsidizes bank efforts to avoid taxation.

The tax laws also encourage banks and real estate companies to continue one of the most dangerous practices imaginable: taking pieces of investments in which they make loans. Particularly in times of "tight money," banks and insurance companies are the key sources of capital. Anyone who wants to build a home or start a business or develop a housing project must go to the money changers. But, despite the tight money situation, instead of charging higher interest rates and fees for their loans, banks and insurance companies will often demand an "equity kicker"; in effect, they are saying "if you want us to loan you money, give us a chunk of the property you plan to develop."

This has two effects. First, it accelerates concentration of power by giving the money changers control over land, housing, and industry to an even greater extent than their economic power affords them. Second, because of the tax laws, equity means that insurance companies can actually make more money *after* taxes than *before* taxes.* Thus, while profits surge upward the control over wide areas of economic life by the money changers is broadened. *Fortune* magazine predicted in 1970 that if present trends continue, "insurance companies may soon be the largest landlords in America."

A further way in which banks act as co-conspirators in the steady concentration of economic power was revealed in a House Antitrust Subcommittee report released in June, 1971. In discussing the reason for the merger wave that concentrated thousands of independent companies in a small handful of conglomerates in the mid- and late 1960's, the report noted "participation by bankers in the mergers and take-over attempts was a characteristic of all companies." For example, within the space of one nine-month period, Chase Manhattan increased its line of credit for Gulf and Western from $500,000 to $14.2 million, and loaned Gulf and Western $84 million

---

* *Fortune's* July, 1970 discussion of life insurance companies as real estate tycoons outlined the potential "tax bonanza" possibilities of this concentration of power. It's complicated, but fascinating.

An insurance company will form a wholly-owned subsidiary as a 1 per cent "general partner" in the real estate venture. The company itself would be a 49 per cent "limited" partner, with the original developers retaining 50 per cent. (This gives the life insurance company a management say without risking a lot of assets.)

Now comes the beauty part: the insurance company, in its limited partner role, is paying off interest on the mortgage to itself (as the parent lender). While the interest income is taxable, the interest on the mortgage is deductible. But the tax rate of most insurance companies on marginal interest income is *30 per cent;* the tax-deduction value of the interest is just about *48 per cent.*

Here's what can happen: say the Quickbuck Real Estate Venture paid the Huge Insurance Company $100,000 in interest. The tax on that income to Huge would be $30,000. But Huge is also a 49 per cent limited partner. So it can deduct its share of the interest—$49,000—the value of which is $23,520.

All this means that Huge winds up paying a tax of $6,480—$30,000 less $23,520—on an income of $100,000. That rate is about half of what a cleaning woman in Huge's corporate headquarters would pay on a wage of $100 a week. Further, if the equity position in the joint venture was high enough, Huge would pay no tax at all on that interest.

to finance a major take-over bid. In return, Gulf and Western gave much of the banking business of its acquired companies to Chase, and turned over many of its pension plans to Chase. The conglomerate's vice-president ordered subsidiaries to move their accounts into Chase branches—and one of the bank's vice-presidents, George Abbot, became a vice-president of the conglomerate, where he continued to channel business to Chase. Further, Chase was often given inside information on prospective mergers, a policy that strikes at the heart, if not the letter, of federal bans on "insider trading" in stocks.

In fact, like many conglomerates, Gulf and Western's constant need for capital—and its consequent dependence on big banks—spawned an explicit policy against small local banks and in favor of the big banks. Gulf and Western's Executive Policy manual stated:

> Operating accounts must be maintained at a major bank designated by G&W. Local banks must not be used unless they provide necessary services which cannot be provided by the G&W designated bank, and [when such banks are necessary accounts] must be set up on a basis of having the minimum in fund balances.

This meant, the House Committee study concluded, "a concentration of G&W's borrowing relationships with major banks located primarily on the East Coast."

Here is a dramatic illustration of the vicious cycle of concentrated economic power of which the big banks are an integral part. Banks supply the capital—"other people's money" —with which independent companies are pulled under common ownership. That ownership in turn draws the company's business out of the small, local banks and funnels it into the very banking giants that encouraged concentration in the first place. And, like Milo Minderbinder's enterprises in *Catch-22*, everybody has a share—if you're rich and powerful enough.

And beyond the use of the lending power of commercial

banks to fuel mergers and thus concentration, the enormous, almost totally hidden power of banks over the American economy through stock control is the most basic kind of concentrated power. As of mid-1971, commercial banks held individual and corporate trust accounts—pensions, estates, and the like—totaling almost *$300 billion:* the world's single largest pool of investable funds. And 80 per cent of all bank trust accounts are controlled by 100 banks—with 19 of the biggest holding half of all trust funds. (Morgan Guaranty Trust, Banker's Trust, and Chase Manhattan among them control $49 billion in trust funds.)

Banks aren't allowed to own stocks directly. But through these trust departments, they control more stock than any other part of America. The voting power means that basic economic decisions are in the hands of the smallest conceivable kind of financial elite. Moreover, banks often wind up in a commanding position over an entire industry by gaining ownership of competing companies through trust holdings. Coupled with the presence of interlocking directorates on bank boards, this kind of control means that the banking industry is, in effect, the hidden hand that rules the American industrial nation: hidden because, under the law, commercial bank trust departments are *not* obligated to disclose what they hold. (One bank, First National City, has done so voluntarily.)

Where do the profits of banks go? In addition to one obvious answer (stockholders) a look at the salaries paid big bank presidents for 1970—a year of recession and joblessness for millions of Americans—gives an additional clue. John M. Meyer, Jr., chairman of Morgan Guaranty Trust, was paid $276,250 for 1970. Richard Cooley, president of San Francisco's Wells Fargo Bank got a *raise* of $51,000. Donald Graham of Chicago's Continental Illinois Bank and Trust got a *raise* of $30,000.

Perhaps the king of the hill was David Rockefeller, chairman (and the largest single stockholder) of Chase Manhattan.

For 1970, Rockefeller earned $976,315 in salary, thrift-incentive awards, and dividends. He also earned $39,000 in interest from convertible capital notes; and, in case retirement was on his mind, Rockefeller could forget any worries about living on Social Security. His pension guarantee hit $116,883. A simple increase on Chase's dividend of 20 cents increased his income by $74,000, thanks to his stockholdings.

But, aside from personal enrichment, bank profits go into investments. And it is their control over choosing what and whom to invest in that makes the banking and insurance companies so important—and so dangerous. Chairman Rockefeller has claimed that "the banking industry has paid special attention to the needs of the disadvantaged." The facts are otherwise: for the $8,000-a-year worker who wants to buy a home, for the credit customer using his Master Charge, and especially for the residents of Watts, Hough, and Harlem, banks are implacable foes of a better life. Along with life insurance companies, they have helped create the ghettos and helped to finance fraudulent business practices.

Anyone who has tried to get a mortgage or home-improvement loan for a basically sound house in an unfashionable but salvageable neighborhood knows the negative impact of bank policy. But perhaps the most vicious kind of bank practice—relating to the quality of life in low-income neighborhoods—was detailed before a Congressional Committee in the spring of 1971 by two Baltimore civil rights leaders.

According to their testimony, overlapping interests enabled the Jefferson Federal Savings and Loan Association to force thousands of low-income families, most of them black, to pay 30 to 40 per cent more for their houses than the fair market price. The bank gave 70 per cent of its loans to a real estate speculator, one of whose employees was on the bank's board of directors. These monies were used to buy homes from white families in "changing" neighborhoods. An appraiser would then value the homes 40 per cent higher than the fair market price—and the appraiser was also on the bank's board of directors. The speculator then turned around and sold the homes—often without improving them—for an 85 per cent markup over what he had paid for them. (In the event of any legal challenges, the bank could know that its defense would be made by a lawyer with the bank's interest very much at heart—because he was the chairman of the bank's board of directors. But that may say more about our system of justice and the real rights of the poor than about banking practices.)

What these facts mean is that one bank used its economic power to force up housing costs for families who could least afford it. But was this just an isolated case? Recent investigation by Senator Philip Hart's Antitrust and Monopoly Subcommittee has shown similar practices by banks in Boston, Philadelphia, and other big cities. And these findings come on top of the Kerner Commission conclusion that insurance companies systematically refuse to insure small businesses in ghetto neighborhoods by "red-lining" an entire community—thus often forcing them out of business.

This is what concentrated economic power can mean: basic, life-or-death decisions over the economic and social life of neighborhoods. With much public-relations fanfare, a consortium of eighty banks announced plans three years ago to put $100 million into Bedford-Stuyvesant's attempts to rehabilitate itself. But only $8 million of that money has been forthcoming; while, for a single commercial office building in New York City, one bank put up $115 million in investments. For other luxury investments, from gambling casinos in the Bahamas to $1,000-a-month housing for the wealthy, banks and insurance companies find money readily and offer it generously.

Banks also perpetuate and underwrite consumer fraud by engaging in a device called "the holder in due course." It works this way: a customer buys a sofa with his Master Charge from a fly-by-night operation. He then owes First National or Chemical Bank $200. If the sofa falls apart, the *bank* is still owed the money. The only recourse for the consumer is to the store, which may have gone out of business or moved its operation. No matter how fraudulent the product or service, the bank is still legally entitled to prosecute the Master Charge holder; and, with thousands of merchants using this credit system, there is no real way the bank can police the stores using Master Charge. Frequently, this leaves the customer holding the bag.

Second, at least one major bank engaged in a flat violation of the 1968 Truth-in-Lending law. In June, 1971, Chemical Bank of New York—one of the biggest in America—was found guilty in federal court of breaking the Truth-in-Lending law; its Master Charge bills to customers conveniently forgot to list the annual finance charge, a listing required (for good reason) by law. And in what is at least an ethically questionable practice, if not one that is illegal, First National City's bills emphasize the "minimum payment" provision of the system; what they do not emphasize is that, if the customer takes advantage of their offer, he will in fact keep an outstanding unpaid balance on which interest will be charged.

The way to curtail the irresponsible, unethical, and greedy practices of the money changers is with federal legislation; some of which is encompassed in Congressman Patman's banking reform bill, some of which requires radically new definitions of what banks and insurance companies may do, may not do, and must do:

ONE   Prohibit all interlocking directorates among banks

This means that a director of Chemical Bank could not sit on the board of First National City, Chase Manhattan, or any other bank or savings association. Such a step might encourage the beginning of competition—and perhaps better service for customers.

TWO   Prohibit directors of competing businesses from sitting on the board of a bank

There is no reason why GM and Ford directors should find so ready a forum for potentially collusive or anticompetitive practices. As it stands now, Macy's may not tell Gimbels—but Sears Roebuck may well tell Montgomery Ward, and U.S. Steel says hello far too often to Bethlehem and its other competitors.

THREE   Open up directorships to a wider group

When banks and insurance companies run each other exclusively, there is a clear danger that each will safeguard the other—that big banks will adopt policies enriching big insurance companies, in return for similar favors from the insurers. Moreover, financial decisions that are critical to a community can be, and often are, undertaken with no reference to the people these decisions affect—even if these people are depositors. John Bunting, president of First Pennsylvania Bank and Trust, has proposed expanding the directorships of banks to include youth, women, blacks and consumer representatives. Here, at least, those excluded *do* have a financial investment with the bank, as well as a direct interest in bank decisions relating to housing, industry, and other investments. They should be given seats on bank and insurance company boards by legislation if necessary. For banks and insurance companies are chartered, serviced, protected, and regulated by government. They cannot collect the profits made possible by public policy and then claim the autonomy of a purely private operation.

FOUR   Outlaw the equity kicker

There is simply no justification for enabling the money changers to use money that is not theirs to gain an ever larger piece of the American economy. Clearly, investments in companies would not be outlawed—but the loan-equity exchange *would* be.

FIVE Close the tax loopholes protecting bank profits

Excess bad debt reserves, favored capital gains treatment of bank profits—such breaks simply add to the tax burden of the wage earner.

SIX Require bank investments in needed housing and for other socially useful purposes

Mexico requires that banks invest a set percentage of their deposits in housing "with a social purpose." Using federal funds to insure against high risks, federal law could require—as it now pretends to do—that banks use their investments in part for low- and moderate-income housing. Banks are chartered by state and federal law; they are protected from competition. The deposits are insured with federal funds against loss. The law should require banks to use some of their funds for the needs of communities, particularly in housing, where public projects are lagging far behind the number of housing units torn down because of the lack of capital.

SEVEN Tax the profits hidden by life insurance companies in tax-free reserves

By using outdated mortality tables and underestimated investment income, insurance reserve funds are swollen by $30 billion. Taxing this hidden profit could produce $10 billion in back taxes and $8 billion annually in tax revenues.

5 ★ Natural Monopolies, Unnatural Profits: Utilities

EVERY TIME an American dials a telephone, or turns on a light switch, or cooks his dinner, or heats his home, the rich get richer and the poor get poorer.

The most basic elements of survival in an industrial society—the sources of energy and communication that we use almost as instinctively as we eat and sleep—are controlled by, and run for, a small minority of the wealthy. Through economic and political power, the utilities are reaping billions of dollars in profits from all of us—frequently in violation of the laws and policies that created and sustained these institutions. And there is little we can do about it, unless the long-neglected issue of control of our utilities is made a core of a new political movement.

The source of this twenty-four-hour-a-day transfer of wealth to the wealthy is the "public" utility—those companies, almost wholly privately owned, that supply the gas, electricity, and telephone service we use in our daily lives. They differ from ordinary businesses in several basic ways.

First, we cannot as consumers turn elsewhere to purchase

the services they offer. It is possible, at least in theory, to "punish" an automobile company by buying a competitor's product, or by refusing to own an automobile. If enough of us make that kind of decision, even the most powerful of corporations must listen: Ford dropped the Edsel, Chrysler no longer makes De Sotos, and General Motors halted production of the Corvair. The same kind of choice is possible in picking food, cosmetics, clothing, and reading matter. But for most of us there is no way *not* to buy electricity or heat, and almost no way *not* to use a telephone. When we talk about utilities, we are talking about necessities.

Second, these utilities are "natural monopolies." It would be foolish to let five or fifteen telephone companies compete for the business of residents and businesses, or to let different electric companies string wires and supply power to a city. Single, unified systems are essential; thus, unlike businesses that must fight with rivals for business, the utilities are the only game in town.

Third, utilities are run without the risk of failure. This is critical to remember: *the law says that utilities must make a profit.* While other businesses feel the pinch of recessions and hard times, the utilities still make money for their stockholders. During the 1957–58 recession, when the after-tax profits of all corporations dropped by an average of 18 per cent, the after-tax profits of private utilities *increased* by 7.5 per cent. In 1970, a year of retrenchment and losses for hundreds of businesses, the trade publication of the private electric utility industry, *Electric Light and Power,* reported an 8.3 per cent *gain* for the year on net income.

Fourth, because utilities are permitted to run as monopolies and without risk, the law requires that they be strictly regulated, and that their profits be limited. It is unfair, the theory goes, to let protected enterprises make the same kinds of speculative profits that risk-running enterprises can make if they succeed. It is up to government regulation to keep profits fair without being exorbitant and to protect the public's right to good service at fair rates.

But like so many other parts of our process, the second half of this economic equation has broken down. The utilities are, in fact as well as in theory, necessities, monopolies, and profit-making—but the theory of government regulation has been perverted into a world of exorbitant profits for privately-owned utilities.

The first but almost invisible fact about utilities is their sheer size. We are accustomed to thinking of "giant corporations" as meaning steel, autos, drugs, and oil. But the utilities are the biggest of them all. The Bell System, which includes American Telephone and Telegraph, the local telephone companies, Western Union, and Western Electric, has assets of almost $50 billion; it is the single biggest private enterprise. It controls not only the telephone, telegraph, and overseas circuits, but the lines through which radio and television broadcasts are sent. Through its link with International Telephone and Telegraph—by itself, the world's ninth largest corporation—it has interests in more than forty foreign countries.

The electrical power industry is the single biggest industry in America. The assets of New York's Consolidated Edison alone are almost $4 billion; nationally, industry assets total $110 billion, far more than those of any other industry. The net income of electric utilities for 1970 was $3.4 billion, an all-time record.

The key importance of the size and pervasiveness of utilities is that excess or illegally high profits for utilities make inflation a certainty. If, for example, the telephone and electric bills of each of America's 70 million households total $5 a month more than they should, it would mean that $4.2 billion every year is being taken by utilities not for any service, but to pay for waste and profits. (That same $5 a month would mean $8,000 over the working life of the average American.) It is that kind of payment without compensating service that is the essence of inflation.

The second fact about utilities is that their operations are shrouded in mystery, and at times in officially sanctioned secrecy. Like so many other bread-and-butter economic issues, the rates and profits of utilities are clouded by technical, detailed matters of accounting understood all too well by the battery of lawyers, accountants, and hired consultants, but not at all by the public that has to foot the bill. For example, we don't really know who owns the utilities—who profits by the decisions of state and federal regulatory agencies. Utility stocks in most cases are held by brokerage houses, and these refuse to disclose the real owners of the stocks. And information about the most basic questions of these government regulated monopolies is hidden from public view.

When Virginia State Senator—now Lieutenant Governor— Henry Howell wanted to learn about the profits of the Chesapeake and Potomac Telephone Company, neither the company nor Virginia's State Corporation Commission would disclose the monthly revenue reports. Florida's Public Service Commission wouldn't let the city of Miami examine the books of Florida Power and Light; and New York City was similarly denied access to the books of Con Ed by the state Public Service Commission.

This is *not* simply an abstract question of the public's right to know. It goes to the heart of whether utilities are making exorbitant profits—a question that can only be answered by detailed examination of where the money comes from and what it is spent on.

To give one example: a lawyer for the federal General Services Administration charged in 1970 that New York Telephone's claimed rate base of $3.58 billion was inflated by some $800 million. The rate base—the capital investments, assets and debts, and fixed costs—of a utility is the key figure from which utility rates are determined. So if New York Telephone's rate base really is $800 million too high, it means the company is making *$56 million in illegal profits* *every year.** This is the kind of question that cannot be answered if the company's books remain closed to lawyers representing consumer interests.

And the third fact about utilities is that their excessive profits—and the exorbitant rates most Americans pay for their light, heat, and telephones—are made possible by the very agencies that were created to protect the public. Sometimes because of deliberate understaffing, sometimes because of flagrant conflicts of interest, sometimes because of simple incompetence, state commissions do not supply any real measure of protection to the public. Instead, they simply legitimize the excessive profits of public utilities.

Our telephone companies are all privately owned, most of them by American Telephone and Telegraph.† Of our electric power operations, three-fourths of the nation's power is controlled by private companies like Con Ed of New York, Commonwealth Edison of Chicago, Arkansas Power and Light, and hundreds more Investor-Owned Utilities (IOU's for short). Many of these are themselves controlled by giant holding companies like American Electric Power, Inc. and Middle South Utilities, Inc.

The remaining sources of electricity are supplied through publicly owned power companies like TVA or municipally

---

* The GSA lawyer charged that New York Tel was computing its rate base by the "fair value" accounting method instead of by the "original cost less depreciation" method. What this means is that archaic, obsolete equipment, which may be worth almost nothing, is given an enormously high value because of the difficulty in replacing it; it's like valuing an ice wagon higher than a refrigerated car. If New York Tel is making 7 per cent a year on its rate base, an $800 million inflated base means a $56 million return every year that it should not be getting. As for secrecy, Alan Novak, who ran the President's Task Force on Communications, observed that "we had to assemble our own base of information. There simply wasn't any data that didn't belong to the telephone company. They were as antagonistic as hell."

† AT&T is, for example, the *only* stockholder of New York Tel. Thus, the entire 1970 dividends of New York Tel—some $202 million worth—went into the coffers of AT&T.

owned operations, as in Jacksonville (Florida), Los Angeles, and several midwestern states. These public power operations have been under constant attack by private power, which claims it can supply "all the power a growing America needs," and which attempts to gain control of public power by persuading communities to sell their municipal plants to private power companies. We will examine later the nature of this campaign to wipe out public power ownership—and how private power has made its customers pay for political propagandizing and lobbying. Here, it is important to examine how the private power companies make a mockery out of public regulation.

Because of the successful lobbying of private power companies against federal supervision, almost all of the bread-and-butter decisions about rates and profits are made at the state level by state utility or public service commissions. Local telephone rates are not set by the Federal Communications Commission; electric bills are pegged not by the Federal Power Commission, but by state agencies. Even the securities issues of giants like Con Ed are regulated not by the Securities and Exchange Commission, but by the state agencies. And that is exactly what the utilities want. For in almost every state, the regulators are not equipped, either as a result of staff, resources, or outlook, to regulate. This common affliction of state utility regulators means that the consumer pays more, and the secret stockholders earn more, than fairness should allow. What are the specifics of these limits?

First, *imbalance*. In many cases, penny-wise and pound-foolish state budget limits leave regulatory agencies crippled in their efforts to monitor the performance of "publicly regulated" utilities. The Missouri Public Service Commission has 24 accounting employees to check the entire utility operation in the state; Southwestern Bell alone has 780 accounting employees. The PSC's 14 chief engineer officer employees are supposed to balance Southwestern Bell's 184. In 1970, the general counsel's office, which had tried to fight utility increases, had its budget cut from $100,000 to $10,000—at a time when the commission had granted $57 million in utility increases in one year. Even at the federal level, private might is supreme; this imbalance was dramatized on December 23, 1971, when the F.C.C. abandoned a probe of AT&T's basic rate structure. It admitted that it simply lacked the capacity to regulate the regulated.

Second, *distrust of the public*. Many state commissions, overwhelmed with the job of deciphering the technical flood of information, actively discourage representatives of the public from participating in rate-setting. Massachusetts, for example, established a consumers' counsel in 1963, to protect the public against fraud in the market place; but that counsel is specifically forbidden from participating in rate-making cases involving utilities. Pennsylvania has the same prohibition; the utilities board wouldn't even let consumer representatives *see* the staff analysis of a utility increase application. When a Colorado lawyer sought information on the power company's profits and charges, he was told that information was confidential. And the Nevada Public Service Commission held that the rate base—the key factor in determining how much consumers pay—was a matter "beyond the comprehension of most consumers. [It is] for determination at the regulatory level by commissioners who are the sole experts in a position to be adequately informed and to pass intelligent judgement." In other words, the public is expressly disregarded.

This kind of exclusion of utility opponents pervades even the federal level. When AT&T and the FCC negotiated an increase in the company's rate of return in 1969—an increase that could enrich the world's biggest company by $100 million to $200 million a year—New York's Department of Consumer Affairs was denied the right to intervene; the proceedings were secret, with no chance for a voice other than that of the company and the commission to be heard.

Third, *exclusion of the public* from the decision-making

process. Nobody expects a telephone company to be unbiased in asking for more money; that's not the way the world operates. Their experts, staff members, and outside hired consultants will present the most persuasive arguments possible for raising rates. The question is, who will present the other side? Who will interpret the data, challenge the expense claims, and probe the accounting practices of utilities to make out the case for the rate-payer?

In too many cases, the answer is "nobody." In addition to shutting out consumer spokesmen, utility commissions frequently rein in their own staff members. The FCC's Common Carrier Bureau was *ordered* by the commission *not* to take on the role of public advocate; to confine itself to technical information. Given the practice of excluding outside groups, this means there is *nobody* to balance the scales. Neither the FCC nor the FPC lets its staff appeal commission rulings on behalf of the public. But if increases are denied, the telephone or power company can appeal to the courts.

The cost itself of fighting utilities often blocks out the public. When VEPCO (Virginia Electric Power and Light), one of the most profitable of all utility companies, increased its rates for electricity, the city manager of Norfolk reluctantly threw in the towel. "It's too expensive, too complicated, for one big city to take on." So, for lack of several thousand dollars, a multi*million* dollar increase went unchallenged.

The same kind of thing happens elsewhere. When Southwestern Bell was raising its rates and Missouri's Public Service Commission was losing its staff, lawyers from St. Louis county considered fighting the rate hike; but county officials told them *not* to represent the public—the $100,000 cost of an appeal was simply too high. In Pennsylvania, the utility commission was charging public interest groups 75 cents a page for Xerox copies of a utility's application for a rate hike. Yet it is the poor and lower-income groups that have the most to gain from such a challenge because they are often the worst hit by utility policy—whether by the requirement of deposits of $150 and $200 to install telephones and electricity, or by the national trend of reduced long-distance fares and increased local phone rates. These are the people who can least afford the costs of a rate challenge and for whom no one speaks when the decisions are made.

Fourth, *conflict of interest* and a *pro-utility bias* often infest the state regulatory agency. With the public effectively shut out of utility matters, the agency itself is supposed to represent the public interest. Yet often it's hard to tell where the private company stops and the public agency begins. When a pro-utility governor is elected, the state regulatory agencies often feel the effect dramatically. Shortly after Ronald Reagan's election as California governor in 1966, a group of utility interests met secretly to select a new public utilities commissioner. The man they chose—a former paid consultant for Pacific Telephone and Telegraph—was fed to Reagan's selection committee and appointed.

Reagan also named as chairman of the Public Utilities Commission John Vukasin, whose deference to private interests was so great that he once argued against interfering with the utility's judgment at all. In discussing a proposal to provide a special tax break for the telephone company, Vukasin, a former Goldwater campaign aide, said: "I question the propriety of a regulatory agency such as this commission substituting its judgment for that of utility management in this unique and complicated field."

Substituting judgment is, of course, the precise duty of such an agency.

The Reagan-Vukasin team went on to gut the once-strong commission staff by ordering the "rotation" of its personnel; men and women with twenty years of experience in studying the telephone company found themselves monitoring small water supply companies, and the Reagan administration slashed the PUC budget, while "suggesting" the elimination of key staff members who had opposed utility rate hikes.

With this kind of orientation, it is not surprising that the commission granted new tax breaks and rate hikes of up to 73 per cent to Pacific Tel and Tel.

Sometimes this kind of bias results from the built-in outlook of utility commissioners. Sometimes it's a question of actual or potential conflict of interest on the part of the commissioners and those state legislators who set the budgets of commissions.

The Missouri legislature, which pushed through a 90 per cent cut in the consultant budget of the state's Public Service Commission—thereby crippling efforts to challenge the arithmetic of the utility—might have been more vigorously challenged by the commissioners if it weren't for the employment patterns of the "public guardians." In 1968, *ten* excommissioners appeared before the PSC as representatives of utility clients. In Arkansas, a majority of state legislators have at one time or another been retained by Arkansas Power and Light; in Texas, during a critical legislative session on the strengthening of utility regulation, there were four utility lobbyists per state senator (the legislation was killed).

It simply strains credulity to believe that a commissioner whose best hope of future employment lies with the telephone or power company is going to be rigorous in disputing the judgment of his prospective clients. And what this means is that the circle is now closed: the *public* is barred, the *municipalities* are barred by finances, the *staff* is forbidden to advocate the public's interests, and the *commissioners* are frequently beholden to private interests. Faced with this pattern, the whole concept of regulation falls apart.

Just how well the utilities have done in the face of this nonregulation is a matter of record. And here, too, the pattern of regulation for private gain at public expense is clear.

First, utilities operate under a "water-over-the dam" theory that would delight the heart of a burglar. It means that any past overcharges are untouchable by either the public or the commissions. (It's true that the rule is the same for undercharges, but by a strange coincidence the utilities never seem to make *that* kind of mistake.) So when the California Public Utilities Commission (pre-Reagan) found that Pacific Telephone and Telegraph had overcharged its customers by $80 million, the courts held that PUC had no right to order refunds. From 1959 to 1968, New York Tel was authorized to earn a 6.5 per cent rate of return; it was *actually* making 7.3 per cent—a difference of $50 million a year. But that half a billion wasn't even taken into account when the telephone company asked for a new rate increase in 1970. The same thing happened on the national level; the FCC authorized AT&T to earn 7 to 7.5 per cent a year in 1967; it actually took in 8.3 per cent—a difference that increased the company's revenues by more than half a billion dollars over a four-year period. But the FCC, while ordering a 4 percent cut in long-distance rates, never suggested any kind of compensation to the telephone consumers for this excess profit.

Second, a combination of accounting methods and a 1954 federal law lets utilities distribute hundreds of millions of dollars every year to stockholders—in the form of tax-free dividends—while socking the consumer with higher rates to "attract more capital." Under the 1954 law, the net income of utilities is computed two ways: one way for tax purposes, another for regulatory purposes. If the regulatory figure is higher, the difference is put *not* into lower rates, but into the pockets of stockholders in the form of tax-free dividends. Since 1954, more than $2 *billion* in tax-free dividends have been given to stockholders—the figure for 1968 alone was $260 million; for 1969 it was $321 million. The important thing to remember is that private utilities, despite their advertising claim to be big taxpayers, don't really *pay* taxes at all—they collect them directly from the consumer, and when they collect more than they need, they plough the extra funds into capital; in other words, they raise capital not from their stock and bond holders alone, but from the consumer. Needless to say, the consumer does *not* gain any equity interest in the company for his trouble.

A third and continuing reason for the exorbitant income of private utilities is the manipulation of the rate base. When a company is permitted, say, 6.5 per cent rate of return, the most important question to ask is, "6.5 per cent of *what?*" If a utility is throwing into the rate base things that shouldn't be counted, or if it's overvaluing its property, its rate of return is going to be far higher than it should be.

New York's Con Ed officially has one of the lowest rates of return of all the nation's private power companies—one of the few that is set under 6 per cent. But its rate base—from which that low return is figured—seems enormously inflated, perhaps by as much as $800 million, as one federal agency lawyer claimed. Supporting this skepticism was Arnold Hirsch, a utility consultant hired by New York City to probe Con Ed's rate increase application, who said flatly, "I've never seen a company with such crooked books."

Con Ed repeatedly paid ridiculously high amounts to contractors (who turned profits of as much as 50 per cent on jobs for Con Ed) and then passed those costs directly to consumers by throwing them into the rate base—a practice highlighted by the disclosure that Con Ed executives were part of a bid-rigging operation with several private contractors. Until recently, its top staff was encrusted with executives, forty-one of whom supervised only *one* employee each; their salaries went into the rate base. The cost of a single project went from $55 million to $150 million—in large part because Con Ed refused to get the federal aid that could have kept the cost down. Who paid for the extra $100 million? The consumers, because it all went into the rate base.

Because of the crucial fact that *utilities never have to pay for their mistakes,* the profits keep going up no matter how bad the service or incompetent the management. The infamous breakdown of the New York Telephone Company in 1969 was not the result of an act of God. In 1968, foremen and supervisors requested more manpower and overtime because of the sharply rising demand for services. The request was denied; in fact, manpower was cut two hours a week in one plant. In 1968—the year *before* the breakdown—New York Tel's own figures show the company underestimated demand by 20 per cent, and installed circuits for 102,000 telephones when the actual requirements were for 300,000.*

New York's Public Service Commission, however, never did any independent checking of telephone company management; this is understandable, since the PSC had a tradition as a rest home for burned-out political hacks. (In 1970, with an election approaching, Governor Rockefeller appointed Joseph Swidler as PSC chairman—a man with a record of being a vigorous FPC Commissioner.) This Commission was so ill-equipped that it had *two* engineers supervising the entire state telephone operations; its rate staff had let New York Tel's rate of return exceed the commission's own limits for decades. And its reaction to consumer protection was expressed by the Chief of the Telephone Bureau, who snapped "the consumerism that's sweeping the country ought to concentrate on things other than regulated industries, anyway." So hard-working and systematic was the commission that at the height of the phone breakdown—with small businessmen losing their life's work because of fouled-up phone service— the PSC admitted that it had "always assumed" it could not order refunds or deny increases for bad service. The law said otherwise. (In fact, the sudden rush of New York Tel to make up for past mismanagement cost the company millions of dollars in overtime, hotel accommodations for out-of-town installers and repairmen, and high interest rates for desperately needed capital that prudent management would have raised during the low-interest years of the mid-1960's. In 1971, the PSC allowed the phone company a $240 million increase in rates—due in large measure to these extra costs).

The pattern of caving in to the financial interests of utilities

---

* So archaic were some of New York Tel's methods that cable pairs— the links between subscribers and central offices—were assigned out of enormous, hand-written books right out of the nineteenth century. No one thought to transfer these critical records into a computer. The result was an enormous number of fouled-up telephones.

is nation-wide. In April, 1969, the Alabama Public Service Commission, with the approval of new member "Bull" Connor of Birmingham civil rights fame, approved a $13 million rate increase for the Alabama Power Company. Its most important component was a $35 million addition to the rate base to include overappraised land. Missouri's Public Service Commission gave an increase to Southwestern Bell of $18 million *more* than the staff recommended; it did so by padding the rate base to include a plant not yet built. In fact, the commission chairman, in a rare moment of regulatory candor, admitted that the PSC had approved a dollar figure first and *then* adjusted the rate base and rate of return to come up with the right amount.

In fact, so generous are the earnings of utilities that one executive was concerned over the size of profits. In citing earnings for the Oklahoma Gas and Electric Company of $1.70 a share, company chairman Donald Kennedy acknowledged they were "almost too good" and said he was thinking of issuing more stock so that the earnings-per-share figure would be brought down to a reasonable level.

With this kind of official subservience to the utilities, it is not surprising that the money they earn is far higher than those "reasonable" profits permitted under state and federal laws. It is important to repeat the essential fact that utilities cannot lose money; they can't fail; they can't go bankrupt; they can't be affected by any of the normal business fluctuations. It's for these reasons that limits are supposed to be set on their profits. But the facts show that in many ways, utilities make more money than they're supposed to—indeed, they make more money than risk-taking businessmen.

The cost of electricity, for example, should be one cost that is constantly going down; and utilities spend thousands of dollars in advertising boasting that the rate per kilowatt hour of electricity is in fact going down, thanks to the generosity of Investor-Owned Utilities. But the real story is a bit different.

In many ways, the cost of producing electricity has dropped dramatically. Between 1945 and 1965, for example, the amount of energy drawn by producers from a ton of coal doubled; and between 1950 and 1966 alone, the cost of production fell by 50 per cent. As Senator Lee Metcalf and his executive assistant Vic Reinemer point out in their neglected utility study *Overcharge,* "with a few exceptions, and regardless of whether a power distributor is investor-owned, city-owned, or cooperative, the price of electricity should be decreasing steadily. Electric power is a classic example of an industry in which mass production and distribution are decreasing the cost per unit." But, as the President's 1968 Economic Report noted, "public utilities have not passed the full benefit of improved productivity on to their customers." The difference between lower costs and not-so-lower rates is higher profits.

And the *real* profits of Investor-Owned Utilities are far higher than the "rate of return" measurement would indicate. Because of the long-term debt structure of utilities, under which many obligations are paid off at very low interest, a 6 per cent rate of return actually means, on the average, a 9.5 per cent return on equity—a very high profit for a regulated, no-fail industry.

But most private utilities do a lot better than that. In 1967, for example, private utilities charged $1.4 billion *more* than they would have under a 6 per cent rate of return formula.* Later figures, using other measurements, indicate equally excess profits. The 1968 net profit of 206 private electric companies as a percentage of gross operating revenues was 15.49 per cent. And for 1970, 100 IOU's racked up *after-tax* profits averaging 15 per cent—and that in a year of recession.

* This total represents earnings and the 48 per cent tax that utilities "pay". Because these taxes are passed directly to the consumer, a utility charges $1 for every 52 cents it wants to keep. Thus, as Metcalf and Reinemer argue, customers pay almost double for overcharges. Every $5.20 kept by utilities for excess profits costs the consumer $10.

The financial community, which knows a good thing when it sees it, repudiates the claims of utilities that their profits are in line. A 1967 study by First National City Bank showed that the return on net worth for utilities was *double* the rate for transportation—a far more risk-prone industry. And in October of 1970, *Barrons,* a conservative financial weekly, told investors that utility stocks were yielding almost 50 per cent better returns than their industrial counterparts: 6.3 per cent as against 4.4 per cent. "Since 1965," said *Barron's,* "utility earnings have risen 24 per cent, while stocks as a whole have declined 40 per cent."

Yet for all this money—all of this profit that goes to stockholders and utility executives *—the biggest success story of private utilities does not lie in their profit structure. It lies in the brilliant public relations job they have done in convincing consumers to pay more for electricity than they have to, under the rubric of the blessings of the free enterprise system. And what makes this doubly impressive is that virtually the entire cost of this multimillion dollar snow job has been paid for by us—the consumers—with a handsome profit to the utilities thrown in.

The private utilities have accomplished this act of subsidized propaganda by taking full advantage of their "cost-plus" arrangement with their regulators. In figuring the profits of utilities, advertising and public relations are counted as legitimate costs. As a general business principle, these are legitimate costs. In practice, it is something else. For, from the founding of the private power industry under the leadership of Samuel Insull in the early twentieth century, private electric companies have devoted an enormous amount of energy and money to fighting every attempt at establishing public power as an alternative to private ownership. Every attempt to bring cheap power to American consumers has been fought bitterly

---

* Stock options—as much as $500,000 worth—are often used to "reward" utility executives, presumably for their skill in earning the company a legally guaranteed profit. Ultimately, the consumer pays the cost.

by the very interests whose pricing and profit patterns denied electricity to millions of Americans: from the Tennesee Valley Authority to Hoover Dam, from the Hells' Canyon fight of the 1950's to the battle over the Dickey-Lincoln public power project in Maine today, private utilities have thrown their enormous resources into political and advertising campaigns against public power. In San Francisco, they have waged eight successful campaigns against a bond isuse that would initiate public power—despite a sixty-year-old federal law that mandated public power for San Francisco as the trade-off for constructing power generating plants for northern California. (As it now stands, the city produces the power, but it is the Pacific Gas and Electric Company that "wheels" it into San Francisco at a huge mark-up.) In Osceola, Arkansas, in North Dakota and Minnesota, utilities have engineered political campaigns opposing public power, and in some cases have gotten municipalities to sell off their public systems to private companies.

And beyond these specific campaigns, private utilities have a fifty-year record of propagandizing the public with the rhetoric of the Right—heavily injected with the proposition that public ownership of electric power is socialism or worse. All through the 1940's and 1950's, and into the last decade, the pages of the *Saturday Evening Post,* the *Reader's Digest, Time,* and *Life* were filled with full-page ads equating public power with Castro, Russian troops, and the Berlin Wall. Expensive films produced by the Edison Electric Institute, private power's mouthpiece, and shown to hundreds of business and civic groups, warned that communism was just a light switch away. Contributions from power companies to such right-wing propaganda groups as the American Economic Foundation, the Foundation for Economic Education, and the Southern States Industrial Council, all helped to swell the propaganda campaign against public power.

And *all* of these costs—from the contributions given to propaganda groups to the films and advertisements designed to protect the profits of the stockholders—were counted in the rate base as *business expenses*. The issue is not whether those who make money off electric power have the right to express themselves; the issue is whether the customers of that power should foot the bill for those costs, as they have for decades. Indeed, since private utilities are allowed a "fair rate of return" on their costs, they in effect make a profit from their clearly political activities: as well as from such "expenses" as country club dues and questionable charitable contributions. (In 1965, Detroit Edison gave $30,000—its second biggest contribution—to Cornell University, which happened to be the alma mater of the chairman of the board. The consumers of Detroit Edison power might ask why that money did not go to Wayne State University in Detroit, or to one of Michigan's colleges.) Instead of the stockholders bearing the expenses of good-will charitable contributions and political advocacy, those costs are passed directly on to the consumer. Only in recent years have some regulatory agencies—notably in New York, California, and Colorado—begun disallowing expenses that are clearly designed for lobbying purposes, or, like charitable gifts, that should be borne by the stockholders.

The consequent dominance of a crucial area of American life by a handful of private companies has played an important and largely neglected role in the concentration of economic power and the transfer of wealth into the hands of a few people whose identity is largely hidden from public view. But the dominant fact of economic life—that economic power always seeks consolidation and expansion—is also true for private utilities. Increasingly, they are seeking to use the leverage provided by their guaranteed profits to reach out into other areas of American life. And the implications are frightening.

The first is the concentration of ownership over competing sources of energy. Seventy-eight of the major private utility companies hold both gas and electric monopolies over their service areas. What this means, in most cases, is that the same decision-makers can shape what kind of heating and cooking fuel an entire area uses. Thus, if the major source of profits for a gas-electric monopoly comes from electricity, such double monopolies raise the clear possibility that consumers will be forced into using the more expensive source of heating. Virginia Electric Power and Light, a gas-electric monopoly, has claimed repeatedly that it lacks the natural gas necessary to supply new customers. But it also stands to make more money on all-electric heat, which boosts heating costs by an estimated $5 a month.

VEPCO also illustrates another clear potential for the abuse of monopoly power. While VEPCO is the only supplier of gas and electricity in some parts of its service region, it does compete with the Washington Gas and Light company for the heating business elsewhere. In an effort to "persuade" home builders to use electric heat, VEPCO offered free underground electric installation; those who refused the package were charged $250 or more for their installations—an amount clearly designed to serve as a penalty for using the fuels (gas) of a competitor. But VEPCO has no *electric* competitor; and no home builder can refuse to install electricity. Thus, an official monopoly position in one area can be used to fight off competition in another.

But perhaps the most blatant use of economic leverage by utilities is their extension into real estate. While utilities are under some federal restrictions, the housing market presents a golden opportunity for electric companies to expand their wealth, to take advantage of their privileged profit position, and to force their product on the public. For obvious reasons, electric power companies favor the use of electric heat; and their real estate operations reflect this. Franklin Real Estate, owned by Ohio Power (which in turn is controlled by American Electric Power, a New York-based holding company) writes restrictive covenants into its contracts with building contractors requiring them to use electric heat. If a contractor prefers to install gas or oil heat, for economy or dependability reasons, he doesn't get to build.

A North Carolina pattern illustrates the "heads-I-win-tails-you-lose" practice of one utility. In 1969, the Duke Power Company was requesting an 18 per cent hike to maintain its profit and attract capital. But at the same time, it was lending millions of dollars to a wholly-owned real estate subsidiary, the Crescent Land and Timber Company. In addition to advancing $20 million to Crescent in 1969, Duke Power sold $100 million worth of land to the real estate company for $24 million. If the real estate company does not succeed, Duke Power can always raise its electricity rates, claiming "setbacks" in its financial picture. But if Crescent Real Estate turns a profit, it will be the stockholders who benefit—not the public in the form of lower electricity rates. Further, Duke Power is in the enviable position of using money collected from a captive public to compete with risk-taking businessmen. (Needless to say, there is no requirement for Duke Power to use a percentage of the capital raised from low- and moderate-income families to build housing they can afford.)

The abuses of private utilities are increasingly gaining public attention after a generation during which it was almost considered quaint or old-fashioned to fight the fat profits of the telephone and electric companies. State commissions in New York, Colorado, and elsewhere have begun to examine more closely the rate claims of utilities; service is coming under the scrutiny of federal and state agencies. The lonely struggles of senators like Montana's Lee Metcalf and Utah's Frank Moss are receiving support and recognition.

These men and others have offered a long list of proposals to balance the scales more equitably on the side of the ratepayer. Metcalf has proposed legislation to create a utility consumer counsel to subsidize public representatives at the state and federal level; other legislation would force disclosure of the *real* utility owners, as well as full utility costs (at present, an unlimited number of expenses for consultants, advertising, and other special services need not be disclosed).

But here, we urge a single remedy for the continuing victimization of the captive utility consumer:

ONE   We urge the public ownership of America's telephone and electric power systems

We have all learned that public control does not necessarily mean fairness, good service, or economic justice for the consumer. Operations like the Port Authority of New York and the Metropolitan Transit Authority are in theory public; but they are still run by the financial elite; the profits still go to a handful of bondholders; and the public gets neither economic nor efficient service. We know, too, that the "public" label in totalitarian nations does not really mean that the people are in any sense in control of the services that affect their lives.

But in the field of utilities, the American experience has shown that public power *is* cheaper and produces other side benefits. In addition to the lower power rates communities like Los Angeles, Jacksonville (Florida), and Springfield (Illinois) enjoy—thanks in large measure to muncipally owned power systems—their utilities actually pump large amounts of money into the local treasuries, which helps keep taxes down.

Private companies fear this kind of example, which is why they work so hard to persuade localities to sell their public systems. (In 1959, Con Ed purchased New York City's subway generators largely—according to the company's own explanation—to reduce the potential for public power in New York City.) Today, new technology would make it possible for a national power grid to be established, virtually ensuring against regional blackouts, with localities operating their own systems.

We believe it is time to raise once again a basic question of fairness: if an operation is a natural monopoly—if competition is not a feasible method of running telephone or power systems—then why should a handful of ultrawealthy institutions and people profit from this? Why should effective control and enormous financial benefits be in the hands of a few? We believe it makes no sense. The stockholders and chief executives have profited enormously from decades of exploitation (in this arena, that overused phrase applies). We believe the next president should establish as a national policy the public ownership of the nation's telephones, electric transmission lines and gas pipelines, and power systems, through a fair method of compensation to stock and bond holders. We have seen already that profit, not ideology, is what counts: when America's passenger railroads were run into the ground by the private companies, the creation of a government corporation—Amtrak—was permitted with no reference to the God-given superiority of private enterprise. There is no reason why a profitable natural monopoly should remain in operation for the enrichment of the few. This is one clear case where "power to the people" is a precise political goal.

6 ★ Them That Has, Keep: Taxes

"Anybody has a right to evade taxes if
he can get away with it. No citizen has a
moral obligation to assist in maintaining
the government. If Congress insists on
making stupid mistakes and passing
foolish tax laws, millionaires should not
be condemned if they take advantage of
them."—J. P. MORGAN

A MAN making $6,000 a year spends almost all of it on the
things he needs to live: food, shelter, clothing. A man making
$200,000 a year has a far wider range of choices: two houses,
three cars, European and Caribbean vacations, servants, private schools for his children. A fair tax system understands
this fact of economic life; that is why a tax on incomes is
graduated—it takes not just more, but a higher percentage of
a wealthy man's income, because the rich need a much smaller
share of their incomes for necessities. A progressive tax is
also a kind of balance. You have your wealth, such a system
says to the rich, but you will help pay for the schools that will
give the children of the un-rich a chance to compete with your
children; you will help finance the hospitals to care for the
men and women injured in your plants and by your products;
you will help pay for the costs of pollution and disease.

That is what is supposed to happen. It does not. The American tax system is a fraud. It has been so manipulated by the

legal and political hired guns of the rich that it *reinforces,* rather than equalizes, the power of wealth in America.

Legalized tax evasion has been written into the legislation, regulation, and court opinions of our tax structure. In April, 1971, two Census Department officials revealed that the *real* tax rate of $50,000-a-year families was the same as for $5,000-a-year families—because the affluent family had so many opportunities to deduct, exempt, and shelter their actual wealth. In 1968, Treasury Secretary Joseph Barr told the Congress that middle-income Americans—those making between $7,000 and $20,000 a year—paid a higher percentage of their incomes to the federal government than the richest 1 per cent of Americans. In fact, he revealed, in 1967, 155 taxpayers who earned $200,000 or more—including 21 millionaires—paid *no tax at all.* (By 1970, there were 301 tax-dodgers in the $200,000–plus bracket.) And those millionaires who did pay taxes paid an effective rate of 25 per cent— the rate that is supposed to hit those with one-fiftieth of a millionaire's income.

This legal larceny flows from the special privileges granted to corporate America and its beneficiaries. In a hundred different ways, the tax law says: "All Americans are equal; but the rich are more equal than others." The pattern of unfair tax advantage is total. A $50 business lunch at a plush restaurant is deductible; nobody pays for it except ultimately the ordinary taxpaper, who must make up the business expense deduction. The $1.15 coffee shop lunch of a clerk or secretary, the $.40 hot dog in a company cafeteria, is paid for by the wage-earner. Even the cost of criminal behavior can be deducted from a tax bill—if the criminal is a corporation instead of a street thief. In the early 1960's, twenty-nine of America's biggest electrical companies were convicted of massive price-fixing and forced to pay treble damages to the customers they had bilked. Thanks to the influence of high-priced, well-connected Washington lawyers, the Internal Revenue Service permitted the companies to deduct the cost of the fines—as an *ordinary and necessary business expense!**

The impact of our rich man's tax system can be seen by looking at the most favored of American industries, the oil industry. Despite the 1969 law trimming the oil depletion allowance to 22 per cent from 27½ per cent, (a cut that made a *real* difference of only 1 per cent according to Senator Fred Harris), the oil industry continues to rack up enormous profits while paying a smaller share of taxes than a badly paid worker. In 1970, the big oil companies earned profits of $8.8 billion—a 10 per cent jump from 1969—and paid an average tax rate of 8.7 per cent. By contrast, a $6,000-a-year worker—earning barely half of what a family needs for a moderate standard of living—paid a federal tax rate of 16 per cent. What this means, in brief, is that one of the most important perceived grievances of working-class Americans —that the "big boys get away with murder"—is absolutely true.

Some of the big companies pay next to nothing—or less than nothing. In 1970, Texaco, with an income of $1.1 billion, paid 6.4 per cent in taxes; Standard Oil of California paid 5 per cent; Gulf paid 1.2 per cent. Standard Oil of Ohio not only paid *nothing* on an income of $66 million, but got a 10.4 per cent *tax credit,* to charge off against any future taxes it might have to pay.

The tax laws also shelter other concentrations of wealth. Mutual savings banks in 1967 paid an effective tax rate of 5 to 6 per cent; savings and loan associations coughed up 15 per cent; and commercial banks paid about half of what the average industry rate is. These bank privileges alone cost more than a billion dollars a year—twice the cost of the appropriation for education vetoed by President Nixon in 1969 as "inflationary." And the tax rate of private utility companies

---

* The 1969 Tax Reform Act limited these deductions substantially by permitting companies to deduct only the one-third of the fines that represented actual reimbursement to the cheated parties.

dropped from 14.7 per cent of revenues in 1955 to 11.6 per cent in 1967.* What these companies do not pay in taxes goes to stockholders in the form of excess profits—and stockholders are overwhelmingly the richest of Americans.

Tax favoritism is not confined to rich institutions; it extends as well to rich individuals. Right-wing polemicists make much of the high rates of taxation at the federal level—theoretically, those with incomes in the top bracket once paid 91 per cent in taxes, and now pay 65 per cent (in 1973, the top rate will drop to 50 per cent). But the truth is that *almost nobody pays these rates because money earned by the wealthy is taxed less severely than money earned by the average American.*

When a taxpayer buys stock and sells it at a profit (a transaction not a normal part of an $8,000-a-year life style) that profit is *not* taxed at "ordinary income" rates, but at a "capital gains" rate—a tax that exempts half of the profit from taxation and that costs the Treasury $20 billion a year. No such special privilege is given to a worker who earns extra money through overtime, or to a family in which both husband and wife work. That kind of earnings is "ordinary income."

When a rich man dies and leaves his stock to his heirs, there is no tax whatever as long as the stock is not sold. All of the enormous economic advantages of stock ownership—power to influence corporate decisions, collateral for borrowing funds for new ventures, and the like—accrue to the sons and daughters of the rich without any cost; it's a kind of economic representation without taxation. There is no such escape for the wage-earner; every dollar he makes is subject to withholding at the federal and state level.

An individual or financial institution with capital can completely escape the force of the tax law by investing money in state and local bonds, which are tax-free, risk-free, and which —despite the low return on interest—actually are more profitable than high-interest taxable investments. (To a tax-

* Banks and utilities are discussed in detail in chapters 4 and 5.

payer in the 50 per cent bracket, a 5 per cent tax-free municipal is the equal of a 10.5 per cent taxable investment.)

"Charity" is another loophole by which the rich dodge taxation. A corporation or family trust can create a foundation,
and can channel the largely tax-free proceeds of this institution into whatever fields it chooses.* If a millionaire decides
that his foundation will support psychic research, or the private school of which he is an alumnus, he can do so and reap
the tax benefits. And whether he decides to underwrite medical research, or community-action groups, it is *his* money and
his choices—all beyond public influence. The wage-earner
has no choice. His income taxes go directly to Washington
and the state. He has no way to disapprove the spending of
his money on projects with which he disagrees. And thus the
tax law further enhances the power of the wealthy: the monies
of the rich make public policy every day; between elections,
the rest of us just send the tax payments to the decision-
makers.

The enormous injustices written into the federal tax code
were underscored by Stanley Surrey, a former Assistant Secretary of the Treasury, in a 1971 paper for the Council on
Policy Evaluation. These exemptions from the tax code, Surrey said, are really "tax expenditures"—subsidies to the
wealthy, which in 1970 totaled $50 billion. Although these
exemptions are offered under the guise of aiding social goals,
the real consequence is, as Surrey puts it, that "we achieve
our social goals by increasing the numbers of tax millionaires."

These hidden "tax expenditures" mean, for example, that
a $200,000-a-year family "gets" a $70 subsidy for every $100
of mortgage payments it makes; while a $10,000 a year cou-
ple gets only $19. The incentives for housing rehabilitation
mean, in effect, that the richest of taxpayers gets a 19 per cent

---

* In 1969, a 4 per cent tax on the income from foundation investments was established, and some controls on the unsupervised abuses
of foundations were established for the first time; before 1969, all
income from foundations was completely tax-exempt.

investment credit, while an average-bracket payer gets only a 5 per cent break. The measure of the outrages legislated into the tax code is that if these kinds of "expenditures" were voted on as subsidies, not a senator or congressman would have the chutzpah to vote for them. But they are just as real as welfare checks for millionaires even though they are buried under mountains of technicalities.

The inequity of taxation at the federal level is, if anything, worse at the state and local levels. Most communities finance their schools from the local property taxes; an inherently unfair method that enables wealthy communities, sealed off from their less affluent neighbors by zoning and construction restriction, to raise funds for their own children and leave the wage-earner and the poor to fight over the remaining scarce resources. States base much of their revenue-raising on the sales tax: a regressive tax, since it makes no distinctions based on ability to pay.*

The inequity of the property tax is compounded by the free ride given to giant "public" or "charitable" institutions in the form of exemptions from the property tax. Nearly *one-third* of the $850 billion of real estate in America is tax-exempt, leaving the homeowner and the marginal shop-keeper, as well as the big real estate and financial interests, to pick up the slack. Some of these exemptions are legitimate: hospitals, purely religious or charitable institutions, and the like. But billions of dollars worth of property that is exempt actually enriches the wealthy; private clubs, for example, in the big city, or foundation offices that would normally be assessed at several million dollars. In some cases, the financial return to the elite is direct, and directly at the expense of the nonwealthy.

* Two concepts many people fail to grasp are (1) an income tax at the state level may be far more desirable for the average wage-earner than a sales or property tax increase, and (2) a 6 per cent sales tax is *regressive, not equal,* since it makes no distinction on ability to pay; the millionaire and the waitress pay the same tax rate on food, clothing, and recreation.

Say, for example, a bank, financial institution, or million-aire purchases the bonds of the Port Authority of New York —an interstate compact with the responsibility for running both the bridges and tunnels between New York and New Jersey and the three metropolitan airports. The Port Author-ity can decide—as it has—to enrich itself by going into the real estate business and building two 110-story kleenex boxes called the World Trade Center. Because they are a "public" institution, no public authority can stop the Port Authority —not the mayor, not the governors of New York and New Jersey, not the city council or state legislature or Congress; not even a public referendum. The Port Authority has total power to condemn the property, wiping millions of dollars off the tax rolls, and to construct tax-exempt giants that com-pete in space rentals with tax-paying real estate businesses. It can lease space for restaurants, shops, all manner of busi-nesses that gain in lower rent from the unfair advantage of tax exemption. The profits from the Port Authority's commer-cial operations—$12 million a year from JFK Airport res-taurants alone—go back to the investors, whose profit is tax-free. Moreover, so narrowly is the Port Authority's financial operation conceived by its directors, that hundreds of millions of dollars in surpluses, which could be used to salvage New York's collapsing mass transit system, are kept in reserve— not for the people of New York City, but for the bondholders. Thus does public authority and private power come together in a massive fusion of wealth that leaves the ordinary, tax-paying New Yorker as its victim. (There is a special added attraction to the Port Authority's situation. The World Trade Center was built during a time when the office boom in New York City suffered a setback because of the recession. Two 110-story *unrented* kleenex boxes would have meant financial difficulty for the Port Authority and its bonds. But Governor Nelson Rockefeller came to the rescue by renting fifty-eight floors of the center for New York State offices. What is one of the biggest financial institutions with holdings in the Port

Authority? The Chase Manhattan Bank. And who is the chief executive and biggest stockholder in Chase Manhattan Bank? *David* Rockefeller.)

As with so many other areas of public life, the question of who wins and who loses economic privileges from the tax law is a political question; Congress and the president determine the shape of our revenue system. And, as in so many other areas, those who hold wealth also control great political leverage. Rich people can be liberal, conservative, reactionary, radical; they may oppose the war or favor equal rights for racial and religious minorities; they may want to fight pollution or cure cancer. But there just aren't that many people who are on the long end of the stick who will voluntarily surrender tax privileges that save them thousands of dollars a year. Consequently, those with protected wealth offer massive campaign contributions in return for the "right" vote to block tax reforms. This strength has produced in liberal as well as conservative presidents a pattern of building inequity into the tax structure.

In 1971, for example, with one of the biggest peacetime federal deficits in history, President Nixon authorized a new set of rules governing capital depreciation that will cost the federal treasury—and therefore the American taxpayer—$39 billion by the end of the decade. This is perhaps no surprise, given Nixon's lifelong career of pandering to the economic interests of big business.

But liberals like John Kennedy and Lyndon Johnson did little better. The tax cut of 1964—originated by Kennedy and passed under Lyndon Johnson—was nothing less than a windfall for the rich. Economist Leon Keyserling noted this breakdown of benefits:

The one-third of American taxpayers who earned less than $3,000 got 3.7 per cent of the cut.

The 1.9 per cent earning $20,000 a year got 21.1 per cent of the cut.

And the one-third of 1 per cent of taxpayers making $50,000 got 8.3 per cent of the cut.

This windfall came at a time when corporate profits had grown by more than twice as much as the economic growth rate and by almost four times as much as a worker's weekly earnings.

The damage to our political system spawned by this pattern of privilege cannot be overstated. A $150-a-week employee may not know the details of the capital gains law; but if he knows that he pays more of his income in taxes than the people who own the plant he works in, that is enough to breed cynicism in the most patriotic of citizens. It has been, too, one of the prime reasons for the bitter reaction of working-class whites against programs to promote social justice. When a wage-earner sees "socially conscious" businessmen promoting government programs for the poor, when he hears rich executives tell him to "give a damn," he knows that given the way the tax system is rigged *those advocates will not be paying their fair share of the program.* His son's job security may clash directly with the demand of racial minorities to be admitted to a union; Head Start centers in ghettos may mean more competition for inadequate openings in a state university in another fifteen years; but however much social justice for the poor may cost the not-quite-poor, the top wealth-holders will continue to evade their share of taxes. In this sense, the growing belief among working Americans that the very rich and the very poor are squeezing him from both sides turns out to have a hard economic basis in reality.

Despite the Byzantine complexities of the tax system—which by itself amounts to a full employment program for the nation's tax lawyers—the theory remains strong that the tax code is not an instrument of social policy, that its sole function is to raise revenue. In fact, this is nonsense. Every exemption, deduction, credit, and surcharge amounts to a statement of policy. We encourage private charities; we believe that those who are blind, over sixty-five, or dependent deserve special consideration. Those are, in principle, unobjectionable social policies.

But our tax law as it now stands encourages—intentionally

or not—a plethora of policies that directly promote the concentration of economic power. The merger wave of the late
1960's was in part the result of companies looking for tax
advantages through take-overs; the absorption of large tracts
of land by corporate conglomerates is encouraged by depreciation laws that enable these companies to sell land at enormous
profits without taking on a high tax load; the growing use by
insurance companies of the "equity kicker"—demanding part
ownership in a development enterprise in return for investing
capital in it—reflects the tax breaks available under that kind
of practice. The result of all of these practices is *concentration*; the use of capital not so much to start new enterprises,
but to absorb old ones. And thus, while our antitrust policies
encourage diversity, competition, and a halt to concentrated
ownership, our tax laws promote exactly the reverse.

The path to reform through the thicket of tax breaks for the
rich is politically difficult, but conceptually simple. Its root
principle is to stop treating money earned through prior
wealth more favorably than that earned through hard work.
It is time to tax the *real* earnings of our wealthiest citizens.

And this can only be done through reforms that close *all*
of the loopholes in our tax law; otherwise, the tax-dodgers and
their advisers will simply move capital from one shelter to
another.

**ONE   No more tax-exempt state, municipal, and indus-
trial revenue bonds**

While this tax shelter may entice investments in local and
state projects, the cost—in terms of money lost to the Treasury
and fairness—is too high. Considering the enormously increased revenues available to all levels of government from
the closing of the tax loopholes, the actual loss of capital

would not be significant, especially given the potential for federally-supplied capital. Further, the enormous cost of debt service now being carried by so many states and cities would be eased substantially.

TWO **A drastic reduction—if not an outright repeal—of the favored treatment given to profits from stocks and bonds**

It is difficult to understand how the work ethic justifies government favoritism toward unearned, rather than earned, money. However much we may admire a man with the individual get up and go to inherit money and invest it in a stock or bond, it is doubtful that he has done more to gain his profit than a man who operates a punch press, or a woman who waits on retail customers eight hours a day. The $10,000 earned when a stock is sold should be counted—and taxed— the same as the $10,000 that represents 2,500 hours of work.

THREE **Taxation of income no matter what the institution**

A church that operates a parking lot for its members on Sundays and runs it as a commercial operation the other six days of the week is entitled to make a profit on that operation. But it is not entitled to keep that income free of taxation. If it seeks to finance itself by running enterprises, it should do so under the same rules that apply to any other enterprise. When a church removes the vestments and dons the sales apron, its special privilege should not remain. The same is true of other "nonprofit profitable" institutions. The American Medical Association earns $10 million a year from advertising placed in its journal. Before that $10 million is added to the AMA's courageous efforts to maintain the $40,000-a-year average earnings of doctors, it ought to be taxed under the same rules as any other publication. If social clubs, universities, bar associations, and charities whose main function is to salve the conscience of the rich want to maintain plush real estate holdings, let them pay the same taxes as a homeowner or ordinary businessman.

FOUR A 90 per cent inheritance, gift, and estate tax

We do not go so far as one suggestion that all estates be wiped out on the death of the original accumulator. That suggestion was made by Andrew Carnegie. But the advantage owned by the children of the rich is now almost insurmountable. Nobody knows whether Henry Ford II, or the DuPont heirs, or the Rockefellers would have attained the positions of power they now hold on their own; for all we know, Henry Ford II might be a burial plot salesman were it not for the accident of birth; or he might be the head of a major motor company. But given the all-important link between wealth and political power, the preservation of estates is equivalent to giving the children of the rich 100 votes at birth, which they cast regardless of ability or wisdom.

FIVE An end to charitable contributions that enrich the wealthy

A taxpayer who buys $10,000 of stock, takes the dividends while it rises to $30,000, and then gives the stock to charity for a $30,000 deduction is in fact taking to heart the adage that "charity begins at home." The same is true of donations of artwork and possessions that appreciate in value; it's a method of avoiding the tax that should fall on his earnings. These and other venerable dodges should be eliminated.

SIX No more depreciation and other "intangibles" write-offs

These kinds of deductions are given without any relation to

the actual costs incurred by a company. Except for the costs that a business actually pays out of pocket, allowances for nonexistent "depreciation" costs must end.

SEVEN **A flat limit on deductions for meals and travel as business expenses**

If a vice-president of a business wants to spend $35 for a bottle of Chateau Margeaux, fine. But his stock clerks should not pay more taxes because of that exercise in good taste. These kinds of expenses—the whole "expense account" form of compensation for the wealthy—are nothing but disguised income, and should be treated as such.

EIGHT **A conscious shaping of tax policy that discourages and punishes increased concentration of economic power, that rewards the less affluent, and that discourages socially disadvantageous policy**

Since all tax decisions promote economic and social policies —whether intentional or not—a fair tax system should consciously promote the dispersion of economic power. For example, a company that grew to market-dominance size, or shared a monopoly with a few other companies, could be assessed an "oligopoly tax" on profits above a certain rate of return. A business attempting to compete in an oligopoly market, on the other hand, could be given a lower tax rate until it achieved a secure foothold in the market.

Along the same lines, businesses that cause social costs— like pollution or disease—could be taxed to help alleviate what they do. Like the concept of absolute liability that governs dangerous industries, a "social cost" tax could devolve on businesses which inevitably increase the burden of others. Auto companies clinging to the filthy internal combustion engine could be taxed on a scale linked to the amount of pollution they cause (GM, responsible for about a third of carbon monoxide pollution, would be taxed on that basis). Strip-mine companies allowed to operate might have to pay a land reclamation tax—an idea already in operation in parts of Appalachia.

Similarly, individuals could be rewarded with tax deductions for actions that were socially important; if overpopulation is in fact a serious crisis in America, it might make sense to grant a tax credit to couples with two children or less, instead of granting exemptions for each child. Or perhaps in urban centers, families could gain a tax credit for *refusing* to own a car.

NINE   The formation of a political movement to force reform

The fight for a fair tax law will be one of the most difficult imaginable. There will be few board chairmen, well-meaning stockholders in big corporations, and other representatives of wealth urging the Congress to "give a damn" about the average taxpayer. Thus, the element of tax reform critical to a populist strategy is an absolute refusal to support congressional and presidential candidates who equivocate on tax reform. The link between wealth and political leverage has cost the American working family billions of dollars that should have been paid by the wealthy. And it has been the venality, cowardice, and corruptibility of our politicians that has permitted this system to continue. Only when the public understands the significance of this issue—only when there are marches on Washington, and speeches to the nation, and the kind of fervor that embraces a political issue with a moral argument behind it—can the battle for a fair tax system be won.

7 ★ The Great American Dream Machine: Regulatory Agencies

In 1893, six years after the Interstate Commerce Act created America's first regulatory agency, sentiment for repeal was growing in the rail industry. Grover Cleveland's Attorney General offered some advice to a railroad tycoon: relax.

> The Commission [the Attorney General wrote] is, or can be made, of great use to the railroads. It satisfies the popular clamor for government supervision of the railroads at the same time that that supervision is almost entirely nominal. Further, the older such a commission gets to be, the more inclined it will be found to take the business and railroad view of things. It thus becomes a sort of barrier between the railroads and the people and a sort of protection against hasty and crude legislation hostile to railroad interests.

Eighty years, and a library full of "reform" legislation later, the advice of the Attorney General is every bit as sound. The corporate giants of America have almost nothing to fear from the agencies created to control private power in the public interest. Instead, by a combination of legal skill, political clout, economic power, and occasionally outright corruption, American commerce and industry now effectively control these government agencies. Regulation has become a fix. And the public pays for the fix—always with its pocketbook, often with its convenience and safety, sometimes with its health and life.

Like so many other parts of our public life—tax reform, foreign policy, industrial safety—regulatory agencies cloak profound issues in esoteric language, secrecy, and dilatory, expensive, almost invisible proceedings. Only when the consequences of these procedures become visible—only when passenger trains stop running, or when the fat content of meat doubles in a few years, or thirty-five schoolchildren die on a twisting mountain road when the brakes of a bus fail—only then do we understand what those commissioners in their elegant offices have been doing. Mostly, they have been helping to enrich the wealthy at the expense of the poor and the not-quite-poor.

The first point to get clear about regulatory agencies* is that *they do not do their job.* If there is one quick way to find out what these agencies are doing, it is to read the laws that created the agencies—especially the parts about purpose and intent—and then asume that exactly the opposite has been done.

The Interstate Commerce Commission was supposed to regulate the surface transportation industry, ensuring fair competition and public service. But over the last thirty-five years, the ICC has deliberately kept trucking rates artificially high; it has blocked free competition; and, despite warnings as far back as a quarter of a century ago, it did nothing while passenger rail service declined by more than 60 per cent in the years since 1958.

The Food and Drug Administration was supposed to protect the public from unsafe or useless drugs and from adulterated food. But for decades, the FDA went after insignificant

* We discuss here *federal* regulatory agencies. For an examination of state agencies, see chapter 5 on utilities.

violators of the law, like Dr. Wilhelm Reich and his orgone box—while the pharmaceutical giants like Parke-Davis, Upjohn, and Eli Lilly made enormous profits on price markups of 3000 and 4000 per cent and sometimes flooded the market with dangerous drugs. (For instance, Upjohn's "Panalba"— a mixture of two effective antibiotics in a volatile combination —threatened the health of hundreds of thousands of users for a good number of years before it was finally ordered off the market.)

The Federal Communications Commission is supposed to grant temporary, three-year licenses to broadcasters who pledge to serve the public interest. But in the entire history of the FCC, only *one* radio or TV station has ever lost its license by FCC action. And commission license grants have led to the concentration of media ownership, in which newspapers and broadcast stations have the same owner.

The Federal Trade Commission was supposed to prevent "unfair competition"—including those mergers and practices by big business that threatened free competition. But the FTC found itself more concerned with touched-up photographs in food advertisements than with the record number of mergers throughout the 1960's.

The failure of these agencies to regulate is matched only by their failure to let the public in on their deliberations. If CBS wants to stop the FCC from breaking up the pattern of broadcast ownership, it has a stable of legal talent and political allies who keep an eye on all FCC procedures—procedures that are buried in the newspapers if they are mentioned at all, and discussed only in the trade press. But if a member of the viewing public, or a citizen's group, wants to object to a station's programming, it finds itself effectively shut out of the FCC—because the commision considers the industry, not the public, its true constituency. (When a group of ministers in Jackson, Mississippi, tried to present evidence of racism and distorted programming on WLBT, it took a federal court ruling to make the FCC even let the ministers speak.)

The exclusion of the public from vital agency rulings is

almost universally true. In 1969, the Civil Aeronautics Board held hearings on possible air fare increases, but the hearings were *ex parte*—informal, off the record, and closed to the public. And for CAB, a California congressman whose constituents would be directly affected by a fare increase was part of the excluded public. The Interstate Commerce Commission has repeatedly attempted to decide basic transportation issues —from raising train fares to discontinuing passenger service —without making any effort to inform the affected public, and sometimes actively trying to hide what it was doing. The FDA repeatedly scoffed at warnings of health hazards from cyclamates—until a new commissioner took office and one morning the people woke up to find that cyclamates were totally banned from food shelves. In the mid-60's, the Federal Power Commission openly rejected conservationist claims that a threat to the ecology of the Hudson River Valley was of any concern to a power plant decision. It took court decision to force the FPC to *listen* to a voice other than the power interests.

This false understanding of whom they serve is the worst failing of our regulators. Out of bureaucratic inertia, or political preference, and sometimes out of straight economic interests, regulators believe that they are there to serve the *industry*—even if a decision that helps an industry hurts the public.

It's not hard to understand why this bias exists. For one thing, industry and agency are a kind of closed shop. They understand each other's language; they are mutually concerned with technical debates that can be more important than a dozen laws; often, they share the same careers. For example: of the last eleven ICC commissioners, four became railroad executives, one became a lobbyist for a group of bus companies, one became a rail freight executive, and three became ICC lawyers, representing private interests before the very agency they had helped to run. This pattern runs through all the agencies.

One of the most pro-industry of all FDA officials, Dr. Joseph Saudek, Jr., became a vice-president of Parke, Davis shortly after leaving his federal job. In the fall of 1971, a high FDA official and one of the biggest pharmaceutical lobbyists simply swapped jobs. The defender of the public against dangerous drugs was now going to fight against "excessive" federal regulation, while the industry's mouthpiece was now going to protect the public!

Rosel Hyde, an FCC commissioner who had voted to protect the media empire of Mormon Church-owned KSL in Utah, joined the law firm that had represented KSL after leaving the FCC. And, in the FCC as well as in every other agency, the lawyers who practice before the agency are almost all former federal officials and staff members with a knowledge of the agency technicalities and good contacts in the government.

With this kind of traffic between private interests and public positions, the consumer has no chance even for representation. The laws that created these agencies all speak of the public interest. But many agencies consider their job to decide between competing private interests—whether in allocating a TV license to a broadcaster or an air route to a carrier —instead of making the general public a specific party to a case. Most agency officials also know that industry is keeping an eye on them: too much independence can mean constant inquisition by congressmen friendly to special interests. The staff people who work for agencies do not have a constituency other than the industry, and the regulated interests are thus free to exert their power knowing that virtually no countervailing power exists to, for instance, support a beleaguered staff man challenging the claims of private interests.

Agency reform is one area where results can come quickly. Two years ago, after Nader's Raiders and the American Bar Association documented the failings of the Federal Trade Commission, swift changes were made in personnel. President Nixon appointed two successive reformist chairmen, Casper

Weinberger and Miles Kirkpatrick.* With the addition of new personnel, the FTC has in two years changed from one of the most lethargic to one of the most activist and public-minded of federal agencies.

Even commission members in the minority can play an important role. Federal Communications Commissioner Nicholas Johnson, one of the freest spirits ever to hold government office, has used the power of commission dissents to express his opposition to the concentration of ownership—and to the timidity in practice—of commerical broadcasters.

These men, and others, have understood that their job is bigger than serving the industry. But as long as the procedures of agencies are secretive, technical, and of concern primarily to private interests, a few good men can make only a marginal difference.

The reforms we advocate would not mean new laws or new institutions. They are designed for what may be the most radical notion of all: the idea that agencies that were created to protect the public interest should protect the public interest. We would reform these agencies by making the following changes:

ONE   Break the industry-agency-industry cycle

Appoint men whose concern for fairness is paramount, even at the expense of technical expertise. Most commissioners are appointed for their political connections, anyway. Technical support for decisions comes mostly from staff. What counts

---

* There are limits to what a president, using his power of appointment, can do. Commission members serve legally mandated terms. If no positions open up, a president is faced with using his influence to provoke an early resignation or going to Congress for legal authority to remove a member or pack a commission.

is the independence of commissioners. For example, former New York Congressman Richard Ottinger was a consistent advocate of public supervision of private power companies. He would be a good appointment to the Federal Power Commission (or, since similar problems exist on the state level, to the New York State Public Service Commission). Lawyer Theodore Kheel, who has exposed the financial interests of the giant Port of New York Authority, could serve well on the Federal Trade Commission (or indeed, on the Port Authority itself). Robert Townsend would make a fine SEC chairman. Nick Johnson, of course, should become chairman of the FCC.

TWO Interpret "conflict of interest" to include more than ownership of stocks or properties in the regulated industry and to carry over beyond tenure in office

Agency officials and staff members should be prohibited for a period of five years from taking a job with any company that falls under that agency's jurisdiction. Similarly, they should be prohibited from practicing before that agency—the Supreme Court does this with its law clerks. Such a ban might make federal officials less susceptible to holding back on judgments for fear of offending possible future employers. The ban should work the other way, too: no employee or executive of a regulated industry should be eligible for agency jobs or commissionerships for a three-year period after leaving his industry job.

THREE Make the public interest a required part of any hearing

Each agency should have a consumer advocate, with his own staff and with his own autonomy. His job would be to represent the public interest in any agency decision affecting either a specific case or the development of general rules. He would be admitted to all agency proceedings as a matter of law; decisions taken without the participation of the consumer advocate would be illegal. This consumer advocate would have the right to issue his own comments on agency decisions, and these would be published as part of the proceedings. Senator Lee Metcalf has proposed such a consumer's lawyer at the federal and state levels of utility regulation. We believe the concept should expand to all agencies.

FOUR   **Make appointments a public issue before elections**

Every politician seeking the presidency should be pressed on the issue of regulatory agency appointments—regardless of whether there is an opening to be filled. The invisibility of this issue has made it possible for rhetoric to camouflage pro-industry appointments that sabotage the very purposes of the commissions.

8 ★ This Land Is Their Land: Land Reform

FOR MOST Americans, land reform is an issue that concerns Latin Americans, or the Vietnamese; its very use in the context of American political debate sounds misplaced or anachronistic, a clumsy adaptation of Third World rhetoric to an urbanized, industrial nation.

Yet the ownership, control, and use of land—in both urban and rural America—is one of the most neglected and urgent questions on our political agenda. The facts are that concentrated ownership of wealth is a reality of life on the land as well as in the corporate world; that hundreds of thousands of Americans are losing their ties with the land, and crowding into our already overburdened cities; that federal agencies, tax laws, and policies have favored the big, absentee landlord over the small landholder; that the indifference to land use has been a major cause of our ecological crisis; and that only a major shift in the way we look at land—an effort particularly by progressive politicians to *think* once again about land policy—can reverse these dangerous conditions.

A good part of the founding American faith was that diversity of land ownership was inextricably related to the health of a democracy. New England town hall democracy grew directly out of the landholding patterns of the region; the contrast between the small-holding patterns of the North and the enormous, feudal holdings in the South was one reason Jefferson was so determined that land be in as many hands as possible. In 1776, he proposed that Virginia grant fifty acres of land to every white male over twenty-one who did not already own fifty acres.

While America is a very different kind of country today, the potential of a large class of small landowners is still great, particularly given the disaffection with city life, the burden on municipal services, and the real thirst for land that millions of Americans still feel.* But while the hunger for land may be reviving, the possibility of land ownership is becoming less and less real.

First, *the small farmer is being driven off the land by large, corporate "agri-businesses."* † The process that began in the 1920's with the introduction of mechanized farming and that has been encouraged by the federal farm program of every Administration since FDR's has culminated today in concentrated ownership patterns.

In 1950, there were 5.4 million farms in America; the average size was 215 acres. By 1970, there were fewer than 3 million farmers, and the average size had grown to 380 acres. The biggest 2 per cent of farms accounted for more than one-third of all farm sales.

In part, this decline reflects suburbanization, and the inability of marginal farms to keep up with rising taxes and costs. But the more dangerous fact is that big business is

---

* A *Life* magazine poll in 1969 revealed that a home and land was the most pervasive desire of Americans; a 1966 Gallup Poll disclosed that most Americans living in cities of more than 500,000 wanted to live in another kind of community, either suburb, small town, or farm.
† This trend and its consequences were examined in a brilliant series of articles by Peter Barnes in *The New Republic,* from which we draw heavily here.

replacing the small farmer and bringing land and farming under the control of a few giant corporate conglomerates.

In the last twenty years, the independent landowners and farmers have been supplanted by giants like Tenneco, Gulf and Western, Penn Central, Union Carbide, Dow Chemical, Goodyear, and Getty Oil. In just the ten years since 1960, the big canners—Minute Maid and Libby-MacNeil-Libby—went from owning 1 per cent of Florida's citrus groves to 20 per cent. And two conglomerates—Purex and United Brands—control a third of green leafy vegetable production in the United States.

Second, the bitter irony is that *these businesses are using federal programs, privileges, and tax laws originally designed to aid small farmers to help drive small farmers out of business.*

For a century, the federal government has tried to help small farmers with a series of programs like cheap irrigation water, exemptions from minimum wage laws, and subsidies for not growing crops. But the corporate agri-businesses are using these same benefits to enrich themselves and make it impossible for the marginal farmer to survive economically.

Federal law, for example, permits farmers to pay their employees $1.30 an hour—30 cents an hour below the federal minimum wage. This law may have justification in the case of a family-owned farm that hires a few workers (and which may well provide room or board, or both, in addition to wages). But does Gulf and Western need federal exemptions from the minimum wage law? Does Minute Maid (a subsidiary of Coca-Cola)? When congressional hearings disclosed that Minute Maid's land was being tilled by farm workers living in wretched conditions, a Coca-Cola executive acknowledged that the disclosures were true and said he was shocked. We believe him; and that is exactly the point about absentee ownership and exactly why federal policy was supposed to discourage it.

Indeed, large landowners have for seventy years been using

federally subsidized irrigation waters in violation of the 1902 Reclamation Act. That law, written to encourage the breaking up of monopoly land ownership, denied cheap water to owners of more than 160 acres. But the law has never been enforced.

Other kinds of federal breaks—particularly in the tax laws —encourage big business to take over farm lands. Buying and selling land at a profit gets treated as a capital gain, while the small, marginal farmer pays the full income tax on his operations. Frequently, farming can be used as a device to "shelter" other income; again, the small farmer has no such break. And, of the nearly $10 billion a year in farm subsidies, the bulk of it goes to agri-business; in 1969, for example, the J. G. Boswell Company got $4.4 million in subsidies; Tenneco got $1.5 million, and the U.S. Sugar Company got $1.1 million.

We believe changes in federal law can both halt the growth of domination of the land by corporate conglomerates and in fact encourage the rebirth of small farming as an alternative way of living in America.

ONE   Use the antitrust laws to prevent further expansion by the conglomerates

The acquisition of large landholdings by conglomerates can be fought through the antitrust laws on the ground that such economic concentration is dangerous to the diversity antitrust laws are supposed to encourage.

TWO   Enforce existing laws

The policy of laws like the Homestead Act of 1862 and the Reclamation Act of 1902 should, at long last, become reality. If subsidized water is not supposed to go to those whose landholdings exceed 160 acres, make that law stick—and perhaps it might make sense to present a bill for back payments to those who have enjoyed the benefits in violation of the law's intent.

THREE   **Revise existing laws to ensure they benefit only those they were intended to benefit**

The kinds of laws that have been perverted from their original intent to protect the small farm and are now being used to aid big business should be overhauled. The farm subsidy limit of $55,000, enacted by Congress in 1971, should be made firmer by plugging the loopholes that now make it ineffective. All such breaks as exemptions from antitrust or minimum wage laws should be cut off once a "farmer's" land and income can be shown to be high enough to take him out of the class of independent farmer.

FOUR   **The federal government might begin to pursue a policy of direct redistribution**

We know this sounds unlikely, and we do not pretend that America is Peru or Brazil. But much of the land now held by quarter-of-a-million-acre giants was acquired illegally from public landholding and in the face of public policy intended to provide small parcels of public land to families that would live and work on it. Without the kinds of special privileges— the subsidized water, tax breaks, cheap labor, and the like— that large landholders now enjoy, it might be more profitable for them to sell their land to the government, which could then resell the land to private, *small* landholders.

FIVE   **Set up federal programs and policies to encourage cooperatives**

Cooperative farming is a means of providing both independent ownership and economies of scale; it means the small farmer need no longer use the outmoded or inefficient methods that have so often forced him to sell out. Co-op farming could be encouraged by a reversal of some of the current thinking now dominating the Farmers' Home Administration.

Up to now, we have been concerned with one specific type of land use—farming. But in America today, land use is not merely a rural question; nor is it confined only to questions of distribution. The larger frame of reference takes in the city and the suburbs, the parks and the wilderness areas as well; it touches on ecological questions—and on issues of social policy. In short, in one way or another, land reform is a vital part of everyone's future.

And that future is not very bright at this moment in our history. For too long now, we have allowed mere ownership to dictate use. Yet, the law has always recognized that the rights of ownership are *not* unlimited. A homeowner who plays loud music late at night is subject to fines despite the fact that it is done on "his" property. A landowner who seeks to build a pulp mill or drop-forge foundry in a settled area will find that if the zoning laws don't stop him, the common law of nuisance will.

But in an enormous variety of ways, the idea of unlimited power to use the land as an owner wills it has brought us to a now universally recognized crisis in ecology. A single developer can acquire and destroy thousands of acres of woodland. The best beach property is restricted either to those who own the land or to community clubs and associations closed to all outsiders. From Long Island and the Jersey Shore to Malibu in California, there is scarcely a strip of accessible beach available to those who lack the money to buy that land. And, while private developers do what they wish to the shoreline and the woodlands—with little thought to ecological balance—the public beaches are dangerously overcrowded, and in our national parks there are traffic jams.

Unlimited power to use land has also brought us to a social crisis. A town, wishing to insulate itself from those without money, legislates two- and three-acre zoning requirements, which means that only the rich can live in that community— and that low- and middle-income housing must be built on the already overcrowded, high-priced property of the central city. And that economic isolation means that the wealthy can enjoy everything from necessities to amenities at the expense of the poor and nonaffluent. Schools, financed almost everywhere by local property taxes, will be better in high-income neighborhoods because the property values that provide the revenues are so much higher; while in less wealthy neighborhoods, the residents simply cannot afford to pay for equivalently good schools, and must choose between crushing taxes and shuttered schools.

This same deadly trap between land control and the victimization of the nonaffluent is true in our big cities. The worthy intention of rebuilding slum neighborhoods led to the partnership of corrupt politicians and land speculators to drive out the poor and reap speculative profits by land development for the middle and upper classes; the experience with New York's efforts at "Title I" housing showed that those connected with Tammany Hall often did nothing but collect rents from low-income tenants of slum housing while neglecting both rehabilitation and redevelopment.

Beyond this, both private and public forces have used their control of land to shatter the lives of thousands—perhaps millions—of people who were living in stable, safe urban communities where a sense of belonging was present. A big land developer's wish for a high school to enhance his property in New York's Queens almost drove out sixty-nine homeowners who had spent their entire lives in a neighborhood they had literally built with their own hands. In Chicago and Cambridge, university expansion drove working-class whites and blacks out of neighborhoods because the ultimate right to dispose of the land was totally outside the control of those who lived on it. The people of San Francisco, perhaps the most beautiful city in America, watched as freeways and high-rise office buildings threatened to "Manhattanize" their city.

And, as the Nader Task Force Report—*Power and Land in California*—demonstrated, land control can serve as both cause and effect of a corrupted political process in which the interests of the wealthy shape the way millions of people live.

What all of these examples illustrate is the danger of concentrating decisions about land use in too few hands. And this is true regardless of whether that decision-making power is in private or public hands. We therefore urge the following additional programs for dealing with the problems of land abuse:

SIX   The democratization of choice about what is to be done with the land is a unified concern that can bring together farmers, urban blacks and whites, and conservationists

Already signs of change in the controls of land are developing. In October, 1971, a New Jersey court threw out a zoning law because it in effect excluded all nonwealthy people; similar challenges are under way elsewhere. The California Supreme Court has ruled the local property tax unconstitutional as a means of financing education because it inevitably benefits the rich; Michigan is already planning a similar court test.

Manhattanites successfully blocked the city from putting an elevated expressway across lower Manhattan and stopped plans to put an eight-lane truck route through Riverside Park; San Francisco blocked the elevated Embarcadero Freeway in mid-air—literally—and citizens are now fighting for laws to stop *all* high-rise buildings from being constructed.

SEVEN   The use of land by private holders must be sub-
         jected to stringent limits

Ownership does not carry with it unlimited rights. We need
to take a hard look at private land uses and determine whether
they accord with the public interest. Here, too, some signs
of change can be seen. For example, the State of Oregon,
following the lead of the Scandinavian nations, has passed a
law forbidding the beaches from being blocked off to public
access.

EIGHT   The most important fight remaining is the fight
         to force the landowners to pay the real costs of
         what they have done and what they are doing

The idea that the destruction of the water and air should be
rescued by millions of taxpayers when a relative handful of
polluters has misused the land is unfair. We believe that the
corporations and developers who have damaged our resources
—who have created "externalities" that damage the health
and well-being of all of us—are the ones who should pay the
cost of redeeming our environment.

9 ⋆ What They Say Is What You Get: The Media

WHO OWNS the airwaves?

Who has the right to use the most powerful device ever known to communicate with the people?

The law says we own the airwaves; that radio and television stations are granted temporary trusteeships over these limited airwaves; that if these stations are not operated "in the public interest," the licenses will be revoked and granted to another group that promises to do better.

Reality is a little different. Just as the law, in the words of Anatole France, "forbids, in its majestic equality, the rich and poor alike from begging and sleeping under bridges," so the law permits anyone to have access to radio and television —as long as he can raise the funds to operate a station, or find the several thousand dollars it costs to speak to the nation for thirty seconds.

The electronic media—most significantly, television—is the most powerful tool we have ever had. Television sets are owned by 95 per cent of all Americans; it is our major source of news and entertainment. If it is possible to pick out a single act, other than eating and sleeping, that most Americans do more often than any other, it is watching television. It is how we find out about the world, about the country, about each other. And, with narrow exceptions, it is accessible only to those with great wealth and power. If democracy requires an open market place of ideas, then what television has become is a company store.

The increasing control of communications by corporate wealth is a fact in print as well as in electronic media. Certainly, we can take little comfort in the fact that there are 1,500 American towns and cities where newspapers are under single ownership; or that print competition in the daily press exists now in only 4 per cent of America's communities, as opposed to 60 per cent in 1910; or that Congress enacted a "Newpaper Preservation Act" in 1970 that legalizes press monopolies, despite the fact that newspaper publishers failed to disclose openly the allegedly weakened financial condition that ostensibly necessitated such an abrogation of the anti-trust laws.

But there is, nonetheless, a key distinction between the press and television. Print is unlimited. There are no licenses, no set number of outlets. The emergence of a challenge to the political and cultural mainstream is not just a potentiality; it is a fact. The existence of important print voices born within the last twenty-five years—*National Review, Ramparts, Playboy,* the *Village Voice, New York* magazine, *Commentary, Rolling Stone, Washington Monthly*—shows that print diversity flourishes.

Radio and television, however, are limited; there is not room for everyone who wishes to speak. And the rules of the licensing game, as they are now played, mean that TV is owned by a handful of corporate giants. They mean, too, that effective, continuing access to television is in the hands of other corporate giants. The law says that first amendment protections apply—subject to the doctrine of "fairness"—to television. The facts say it is the rich and the powerful in

America who get to tell Americans what they should be thinking. For the powerless, and for the ordinary American, access to the media comes only with dramatic, even violent upheaval. The day-to-day concerns of most Americans are effectively shut out of their own living rooms.

Ask again, who owns the airwaves? As far as what 95 per cent of Americans see on television, the answer is: three huge conglomerates. The National Broadcasting Company is owned by the Radio Corporation of America (RCA, Inc.). RCA is also a major defense and space contractor, a washing machine and dishwashing manufacturer, and the owner of Random House, Pantheon, and Knopf books.

The Columbia Broadcasting System also controls $21 million in the credit affiliates of Ford, GM, and Chrysler, television stations in the Caribbean and Latin America, Creative Playthings, Columbia Records, and the New York Yankees.

The American Broadcasting Company also owns 399 theaters, ABC-Paramount Records, three farm papers, and— until it was aborted in 1968—was about to merge with International Telephone and Telegraph, one of the ten biggest corporations in the world, with financial interests in forty countries.

At the level of individual station ownership—where control is greatest and profits biggest—concentration is even narrower. The three TV networks each own and operate five stations in the biggest, most lucrative media markets. The other owners are equally flush, as this passage from a 1968 *America* article notes:

> Twenty-five percent of all television stations are controlled by newspapers. *Every* commercial VHF television license in the top ten U.S. markets is controlled either by a network, a group owner, or a metropolitan newspaper chain. In the top twenty-five markets there are 97 stations. Fifteen of these ninety-seven are network owned. Over half of all television revenue . . . regularly goes to these fifteen stations and their network owners.

Below the level of network ownership, conglomerate control of television stations is still a fact of life. Of the six major nonnetwork owners, five—owning a dozen or more stations —include corporate conglomerates with direct financial interests in critical areas of American life: areas now subject to growing debate.* The concept of an independent voice observing and commenting on conflicting interests is a joke in the television industry; however detached the voices that speak to us from television may try to be, however honorable they are, these voices are ultimately in the control of forces with a direct interest in the present distribution of wealth and power.

The concentration of *ownership* is duplicated by the concentration of *access*. It is not quite so narrow; anyone who wishes to speak to thirty million Americans can do so—providing, of course, he has $60,000 to buy a minute of time on the "Flip Wilson Show," and provided he does not wish to deliver an explicitly political message (political advertising is permitted, with very few exceptions, only for the promotion of candidates; a group simply wishing to argue against the war in Vietnam cannot even buy time even if it has the money to do so).

What this means is that the centers of economic power in reality control the media, using television to sell their products; but what is rarely understood is that this commercial

---

* The firms are: *Avco Corp.,* which, in addition to its financial services, manufactures airplane and industrial engines and parts, aircraft frame components, missile and space products, defense and industrial electronics, and weapons and ammunition; *Fuqua Industries, Inc.,* which is in photo processing and trucking, agricultural equipment manufacturing, mobile homes and land-clearing equipment, motion picture theaters, and real estate; *Chris-Craft Industries, Inc.,* which has interests in auto interior textile plants, cotton and jute pads, rubber products, marine motors, and chemicals; *Cox Enterprises, Inc.,* which publishes newspapers and trade journals, runs common-carrier microwave facilities and motion picture production equipment; and *E. W. Scripps Co.,* which is a big newspaper publisher and owns United Press International, United Features Service, and Community Antenna TV interests.

enterprise may have profound political and social implications. We recognized this in the late 1960's, when the Federal Communications Commission extended the fairness doctrine —requiring a fair presentation of all points of view on important issues—into the commercial field for the first time by stipulating that antismoking ads be put on television free of charge.

But the fairness doctrine has *not* been extended to the endless kinds of commercial messages that shape our political beliefs every day. If General Motors wants to advertise a Corvair, or an automobile that pollutes the atmosphere, all it needs is the money. A group wishing to argue that the automobile is a deadly weapon whose use should be restricted gets neither free nor purchased time—that is a "political" issue.* Banks, insurance companies, oil companies, all can purchase time—written off as a business expense—to argue that they are concerned, generous, right-thinking citizens; a case that banks ignore ghetto neighborhoods, or that the oil import quota costs the average American $50 to $100 a year, or that insurance companies arbitrarily cancel policies, is at best buried in a Sunday "public affairs" show. The average American never hears those cases on prime-time television.

This restricted use of television does *not* mean that nothing controversial gets on the air. CBS in particular, with such

---

* In the summer of 1971, a federal Court of Appeals in Washington ruled that advertising for high-powered automobiles and for leaded gasolines were both "controversial" issues, on which environmentalists were entitled to air time for a response. That same court held that television stations had a first amendment duty to provide access for the airing of controversial items like the war in Vietnam. The Nixon Administration's response to these and other demands for access has been to come down foresquare on the side of money. Clay Whitehead, director of the President's Office of Telecommunications, has proposed scrapping the fairness doctrine, and replacing it with a rule requiring stations to sell time on a first-come, first-serve basis. What this does to community groups or individuals without the money to purchase time is to take away the one chance they now have for access, the "fairness" doctrine.

shows as "Hunger in America" and "The Selling of the Pentagon," as well as Ed Murrow's classic "See It Now" show on Senator Joseph McCarthy, has demonstrated that television can be used to probe and expose.

The question is more fundamental and structural than whether an occasionally challenging show gets on the air. It is whether television provides groups that do not have great economic power with access to use this incredibly powerful medium.

Part of the problem is economic; putting aside the Sunday morning public affairs shows, which rack up "Brownie points" with the FCC, network shows either make money or go off the air. The heralded "CBS Reports" and "See It Now," and NBC's "Project 20," all were once regular prime-time features. They no longer exist. Because of the profit motive, television must try to reach most of the people most of the time. And what this tends to do, apart from reducing most prime-time entertainment fare to mush, is to legitimize the political perceptions of the majority, while shutting out the rest of Americans.

Thus, "The Smothers Brothers" show, with its antiwar skits and occasional satires of political leaders, was immediately considered a "controversial," even "offensive" show. But when, in the fall of 1967 at the height of the debate over the war in Vietnam, Bob Hope came on the air with a show from Vietnam in which he praised the war effort and jokingly approved a division's motto, "If it moves, shoot it," this was considered acceptable prime-time entertainment. There was no fairness doctrine, no equal time for those opposing the war. A group of radical historians seeking to present a "revisionist" history of America in songs and skits would almost certainly be denied television time. But a show featuring patriotism *à la* John Wayne becomes the most expensive TV special ever staged. In the fall of 1970, the American Broadcasting Company refused to show the halftime performance of the University of Buffalo band because its antiwar and ecology themes were "political." But that same Saturday, viewers watched a militaristic salute to America, and all season the three networks offered hypes for the Nixon administration's Prisoner of War campaign, and pregame salutes to the heroes of the Sontay prison raid into North Vietnam.

Indeed, the content of television entertainment offers a revealing picture of who is excluded from television. With the rise of black anger in the 1960's, we became aware that television had shut the black out from its vision of what the world is like; in a few short years, blacks turned up in commercials, on news programs, and on the whole spectrum of entertainment. Yet, all through the 1950's and 1960's as the demand for black equality was rising, blacks were depicted on television from the viewpoint of the white world's stereotype: Beulah, the perplexed but happy-go-lucky maid in a typical white suburb; George, the bug-eyed, lobotomized elevator operator in the all-white building where Vern and Margie Albright lived; "Amos 'n' Andy," which ridiculed the very concept of a black lawyer or community group, and which featured Lightnin—the bug-eyed, lobotomized, lazy porter. Only the riots brought reform to the lily-white world of television.

The man who worked with his hands was also short changed; a dolt incapable of the simplest exercises of the mind, he was epitomized by William Bendix in "The Life of Riley." Women—seen exclusively through the eyes of men—were irresponsible, childish, jealous, covetous, gossipy, redeemed by "women's intuition," which substituted for logic. And perhaps most startling, the ordinary American family, composed of people trying to get by as best they could, was almost ignored, except in the most sanitized, sentimentalized forms ("Ozzie and Harriet," "Father Knows Best"). Detectives, cowboys, cops—all had serious problems; but, except for the radio holdovers of early television like "The Goldbergs" and "I Remember Mama," ordinary people were happy people with happy problems.

The use of television for entertainment and amusement

is a legitimate use; we do not deny the fact that wit, thought-fulness, and at times brilliance has found its way into prime-time television, or that television news has at times given lessons to print journalists in how to inform people about important issues.

Our challenge is more basic. It goes to the heart of how television is structured; who runs the networks and stations; and how television can be opened up to people without great wealth and power. It is not enough to rely on the good will, or honesty, or courage of the few who do have a voice in the use of television. The Constitution is a skeptical document; it is based on the presumption that the potential for the abuse of power is itself an evil and that power should be dispersed. When it comes to questions of speech and press, the Constitution trusts no one with control over such potentially disastrous power, preferring instead to confer the power to speak and advocate on every one of us.

That is the central question we face in watching how television performs; *not* whether the people who run it mean well, but whether they should control such enormous power in the first place. Maybe Time, Inc.—which owns radio and television stations and cable TV—will fearlessly examine the practices of commercial banks; maybe the fact that Chemical Bank and the First National Bank of Chicago own large chunks of Time, Inc. will make no difference. But human nature—the same human nature understood by the framers of the Constitution—entitles us to be skeptical.

The most long-term important issue we will continue to face about television—long after the bullying of Spiro Agnew is forgotten—*is how to diversify control of television in America.* How do we disperse control—control that, though it is held by "liberal" and "conservative" forces alike, is none-theless held by a comparative handful of Americans?

The traditional method envisoned by the Federal Communications Act—that of challenging licenses—is practically out of the question. Congress and the Federal Communications Commission have almost always acted to protect the licensees from attack—treating them as though they were owners, rather than temporary trustees, of the airwaves. In the entire history of the FCC, no station *ever* had its license revoked; and, when the FCC finally acted to transfer control of Boston station WHDH, Senator John Pastore promptly introduced a bill in Congress requiring the commission to show favoritism toward the current license holder in any proceeding. If enacted, Pastore's bill would have totally scrapped the original concept of the law—that a challenger with better ideas and capabilities of serving the public ought to be favored. Only a partial adoption by the FCC of the Pastore view prevented the bill from passing.

When challenges are permitted, they are lengthy, costly proceedings. In New York City, a citizens group, Forum Communications, challenged the license of Channel 11, WPIX—owned by the New York *Daily News,* which in turn is part of the Chicago *Tribune* ownership, which itself holds radio and television licenses in Chicago. The evidence showed that Channel 11 had offered almost no news or public affairs programming, had lied about the location and dates of news film it was showing, had ordered that black teenagers not be shown during a dance show, and had virtually ignored New York's racial and ethnic minorities. The challenge was supported by former television executives, public officials, entertainers with broadcast experience, and community groups—a distinctively impressive collection of talent.

Yet even this relatively well-placed group of applicants has had to wait two years for a hearing, and the final decision will be years in coming. (And during those hearings, the *Daily News* distorted AP news reports of the proceedings in such a way as to favor the station it owned.) The time and cost of such proceedings guarantees that a group of average-income Americans could not possibly mount an effective challenge to a radio or TV station backed by the economic clout of a corporate conglomerate. These stations have the resources to wait out any challenge, and the political connections to protect themselves. And, even while the license is being challenged, the licensees still rake in the tremendous profits of TV stations. This process in effect builds in protection for the powerful and shuts out those without wealth and power.

The alternative to licensing challenges is public broadcasting: television financed by a combination of government, foundation, and viewer contributions. As it now stands, America has a National Educational Television network, a Corporation for Public Broadcasting, and a Public Broadcasting Service. While these new sources of television are welcome, and while they have offered outstanding examples of drama, entertainment, and education, we are skeptical of the long-range chances for public broadcasting to alter the power structure of television without other, more fundamental reforms.

We are skeptical first because there are a limited number of VHF stations—still the key to television viewing—and this means that only one station per city *at most* will provide an alternative source of television. In many cities, including such metropolitan areas as Washington, D.C. and Boston, public television is available only on UHF—which requires a separate dial that must be fine-tuned, rather than clicked into place.

Second, there is no tradition in this country separating funding from control. Congressmen who offer the loudest speeches about the specter of socialism and government control are usually the first to protest any show of independence by a government-funded project, whether a legal services program or a television station. And the Nixon administration has already shown its willingness to politicize public television. In November of 1971, Clay Whitehead threatened the Public Broadcasting Service by promising no permanent financing as long as public broadcasting was unwilling to be what the administration wanted it to be. There is no particular reason to think a Democratic administration would be any more willing to tolerate an independent, government-funded service. And Congress is already deeply suspicious of the activities of foundations, an alternative source of funding. The best guess we have is that public television in America will tend to develop more along the lines of French TV —subservient to the government in power—rather than along the lines of the largely independent British Broadcasting Service. (Even the national BBC is not ideal; the real recipient of public funds should be *local* stations, with a requirement for public access by groups now shut out of any relation with television except as passive viewers.)

The key to real reform lies in diversity—in breaking the stranglehold on TV ownership by those who already have a voice in the community and by great corporate power. As much as possible, we must diversify control over the airwaves.

We think the following reforms could help redistribute power more broadly:

ONE   Prohibit absolutely any owner of a newspaper from owning a radio or television station in his own city

If a Chicagoan distrusts the *Tribune,* he should not, when he turns on his radio or TV, have to listen to the voice of that same ownership on WGN. Conservatives who are dissatisfied with the *Washington Post* and its policies now have a handful of TV stations to choose among, but one of the most powerful is owned by the *Post.* This pattern repeats itself all over America.

If this kind of concentrated ownership were disallowed completely, the dispersal of news access would be increased. It is hypocrisy to say no one else has the money, because radio and TV stations are so profitable that any kind of community group could find money from a lot of small investors *if* the FCC followed the law and treated licenses as trusteeships, rather than as quitclaim deeds. Further, newspapers would not be barred from operating a radio or TV station in another city, so long as their conglomerate network was not already in that city. This would mean that, for instance, Washington and Chicago papers could buy stations in each other's city—thus giving citizens a chance to hear something different.

TWO   Require that community groups be given time on any cable television system

Cable TV is going to revolutionize television. A single cable system can bring dozens of channels into a person's home. This system cannot be allowed to fall into the hands of corporate giants like Westinghouse, CBS, or Time, Inc. But that is just what has already begun to happen.

Instead, the diversity promised by cable TV should be seized on by the FCC—as Commissioner Nicholas Johnson has already proposed—to open up access to television. Community groups of a certain size could, by petition, win the right to air time; once they qualified, a cable system's technical staff could be required to given them assistance as a condition of the original license. This means that in a city, landlords and tenants could debate housing laws; doctors and patients could each produce their shows expressing their attitudes toward hospital care and doctor's bills. The concept of a town hall democracy in which every citizen gets the chance to have his say is itself a real possibility once we make the commitment to disperse the power to be heard.

THREE   Require congressmen to divest themselves of all interests in radio and television

Today, dozens of congressmen own interests in radio and TV stations and more work for law firms with such clients. The possibilities for corruption and conflict of interest are too great to permit this situation to continue—particularly since Congress ultimately controls the FCC, which in turn decides who gets and keeps licenses. To protect the public, congressmen must be taken completely out of the business of licensed media.

FOUR **Turn over partial control of the media to organizations independent of the networks**

Today, a few men in New York decide what does and does not get on television networks. For all practical purposes, they are the arbiters of American taste. Regardless of whether you turn on Channel 9 in Washington or Channel 4 in Pittsburgh, you are watching—almost without exeception— programs chosen by the same group of men.

This is not a fixed principle of broadcasting. In Holland, for example, any group of 15,000 people can organize a "TV station." There, as in many countries in Europe, the citizen pays a broadcast tax. In Holland, the twist is that citizens can then sign a petition turning their broadcast tax over to a particular group—and such a group gets two or four or eight or more hours a week, depending on the number of people supporting it. If interest in programming drops, a "station" loses its access—and thus a pure market test is what decides who gets on the air. The Dutch can turn on programs produced, written, and controlled by groups of conservatives, liberals, radicals, and cultural anarchists—each of whom has its own offices and its own technicians, paid for by the tax of interested citizens.

This means that instead of a single controlling group programming dozens of hours a week, different groups representing, say, labor, housewives, veterans, businessmen, rock music freaks, and abstract artists, would each have the chance to watch and listen to what they care about. It could go a long way toward opening up the media in America.

10 ★ The Great Cop-Out: Crime

No POLITICAL faction has been talking sense about crime. The loudest advocates of "law and order" frequently promote policies that increase the crime rate. The self-professed humanitarian politicians often pretend that crime is an "undignified issue" or an insult to the dispossessed—the very class of people that bears the brunt of muggings, rapes, purse-snatchings, burglaries, and murders.

No issue has proven a more fertile breeding ground for hysteria, cheap political shots, and outright lies. And we will not begin to solve the real issue of unsafe streets until politicians begin to talk honestly about crime.

Richard Nixon has been one of the shrillest voices of hypocrisy in the field of crime. In his acceptance speech at the 1968 Republican National Convention, Nixon ignited a tumultuous roar of delight when he promised to appoint "a new Attorney General" to end crime in the streets. He kept the first part of that promise.

But during 1969, violent crimes in the United States increased by 12 per cent, according to the "new Attorney

General." In 1970, the "new Attorney General" reported another national increase of 11 per cent in violent crimes. On September 30, 1971, the "new Attorney General" announced that violent crimes had gone up another 11 per cent in the first six months of 1971, marking a 34 per cent rise in thirty months.

President Nixon's approach to crime, both in his campaign and as president, typifies the right-wing stance: find a scapegoat—the courts, or political radicals, or an Attorney General who thinks the Bill of Rights means what it says—and link that scapegoat to liberals in order to win votes. In recent years, the Right has equated political dissidents—William Kunstler, Abbie Hoffman, student activists, black militants—with the steady rise in violent crime. It is a convenient handle, striking at a growing sense in this country that security, along with traditional values and standards, is collapsing. The speeches are fiery and brave-sounding; but no one has proved that a political speech has ever frightened a mugger into turning himself in, or prevented a single crime.

When the Right is in power—when it has to *do* something about crime instead of simply denouncing it—its programmatic fights are weak and ineffective. The laws passed with so much fanfare by state legislatures and Congress—preventive detention and "no-knock" laws—frequently do nothing but sanction what police have long done anyway, or legitimize what has always happened to poor suspects who cannot afford bail. But the crime rates do not go down.

Consider Los Angeles: a laboratory for the right-wing's notions about crime. If America has Richard Nixon as its president and John Mitchell as attorney general, California has Ronald Reagan as governor, and Los Angeles has Sam Yorty as its mayor. The California attorney general and the Los Angeles district attorney battle the local police chief to see who can denounce criminals more forthrightly. Not a speck of executive softheartedness taints the criminal justice system. But the city has three times the over-all violent-crime rate of New York City.

The liberal response to crime has been divided. Some liberals have followed Eugene McCarthy's example in 1968; they have tried to make believe crime is not a real problem. This group is frequently a paradigm case of elitism. They live in affluent, all-white suburbs or in high-rise, high-rent apartments with doormen and television cameras guarding the lobby. And, like Senator McCarthy, they argue from their purchased safety that any mention of crime is a codeword geared to getting the votes of bigots. They do not venture into neighborhoods like New York's Crown Heights, where shopkeepers earning a fifth of their incomes keep doors locked during shop hours for fear of armed robbery.

The other liberal response has been to embrace the most facile solutions and slogans of the Right. Many liberals campaigning for office in 1970 adopted this tactic. Adlai Stevenson III, running for Senator from Illinois, named Chicago Eight prosecutor Tom Foran as cochairman of his campaign, and argued that he had sponsored antibomb legislation in the state legislature before his opponent. Hubert Humphrey, in the course of winning back his Senate seat, repudiated his former support for strong gun control laws, explaining that he had fallen victim to emotionalism in the wake of the shootings of Martin Luther King and Robert Kennedy. A majority of congressional liberals voted for the repressive measures in the District of Columbia crime bill.

In both cases, however, liberals have conceded the premises of the Right: they have said either, "you're right, but we don't want to be racists," or else, "me, too, I'm as tough on crime as you are." Neither class of liberals has challenged the Right on the essential ground: that its solutions are not only repressive, but at best ineffective and at worst subversive of real efforts to stop crime.

The attitude of the New Left has been equally unconstructive, for different reasons. Revolutionary student literature, while filled with analyses of the Albanian line and sympathy for the oppressed radicals of Ceylon, has ignored crime as a burden carried by the American poor. Students have marched for a hundred worthy causes, but never for specific programs against crime.

A good part of this failure can be traced to one of the most dangerous trends in "radical" thought: romanticizing all criminals, while abusing all policeman as "pigs." Most student radicals, dazzled by the excitement of real (as opposed to rhetorical) lawbreaking, simply do not see crime as an injustice primarily against the powerless. Abbie Hoffman can publish a book that hails stealing and shoplifting as a superior lifestyle; the fact that a factory worker or welfare mother pays for the higher costs to cover shoplifting doesn't bother him. In his book *Do It,* Jerry Rubin urges kids to kill their parents and blow up their schools. (Since Rubin does not practice what he preaches, maybe he should call his next book *YOU Do It.*) One plank of the Black Panther platform defines all black prisoners as "political" and demands their release—presumably so that these "political" victims may express their "political" bent by beating up sixty-five-year-old black women.

Sections of the New Left and the underground press even tried to elevate Charles Manson into a cult figure—forgetting that, in their own terms, he happened to be a racist and male chauvinist in addition to being a psychopathic murderer. The kind of thinking that invests every lawbreaker with an aura of guerrilla warfare against the state and defines every penitentiary inmate as a political prisoner is so estranged from reality as to approach political insanity. And, even in its milder forms, such thinking reflects a strong strain of elitism. Many student radicals come from middle- and upper-class families; their indifference to crime—and their enthusiasm for lawbreakers of every stripe—reflects an ignorance of the real danger that criminal actions pose to the working-class and the poor.

We share the belief that the fundamental sources of crime are rooted in the pathology of poverty: jobless, purposeless men and women, broken families, a school system that does not educate, and the consequent epidemic of alcoholism and drug addiction. "The slums of the great cities are the breeding grounds of crime," Anatole France said, and that view is still sound. We agree, too, that the failure to punish the crimes of the rich—tax-evasion, pollution, violation of health and safety laws—is a source of disrespect for the law.

But to say this is only a part of the problem of crime. There are immediate steps that must be taken if crime—and the fear of crime—are to be brought under control. People who are afraid to go out for a quart of milk after the sun sets are themselves victims of oppression; and, like all such victims, they are understandably fed up with rhetoric—in this case, rhetoric about one day abolishing poverty as a way of making their neighborhoods safe. We need to take these steps now for the sake of controlling violent crime—which is a legitimate end in itself:

ONE   **Strict federal control of firearms and ammunition is an absolute necessity**

The most obvious piece of legislation which can directly reduce violent crime is not preventive detention, no-knock laws, or permissive wiretapping. It is federal gun control legislation, requiring the registration and licensing of every handgun in America and stringently limiting the sale of guns and ammunition of every type. This is one area where local action is not enough; strict local laws in New York and Chicago have proven ineffective because guns are readily available in neighboring cities and states.

The correlation between homicides and casual access to guns seems indisputable. All the Western democracies and Japan have strong national gun legislation—and far fewer murders than America. Philadelphia—the city of brotherly love and Frank Rizzo—had more homicides in 1970 than England, Scotland, and Wales combined. In that same year Tokyo, with more than 11 million people, had *three* homicides by handgun; New York, with 8 million people, had 538 homicides by pistol—its strong gun laws wiped out by open markets in other localities. (Tokyo's 213 murders by all methods is less than one-fifth the total for New York —1,117.)

In many cities, the "Saturday Night Special" is the favorite tool of murderers: six-shot, low-calibre, $15 guns that are imported piece-by-piece and reassembled in America thanks to a loophole in the 1968 Gun Control Act. Of the ten New York City policemen murdered in the first half of 1971, eight were killed with Saturday Night Specials. These guns have no value to the hunter or sportsman. Their only value is to the potential killer.

Despite the well-organized, politically ruthless gun lobby, and despite the neurosis that leads some men to equate their guns with their manhood, most Americans—70 to 80 per cent—favor tougher gun laws. Police chiefs like Jerry Wilson of Washington and Patrick Murphy of New York have backed Senator Birch Bayh's bill to outlaw the sale of Saturday Night Specials. But America's two biggest shills for "law and order," Attorney General Mitchell and FBI Director J. Edgar Hoover, have refused to endorse any new national gun control legislation. (Murphy and police chief spokesman Quinn Tamm were barred from an FBI meeting on police safety in the spring of 1971 because of their calls for gun control.) When two policemen were murdered with handguns in Harlem, President Nixon went on television to express his sympathy and to propose federal grants of $50,000 to the families of murdered cops. But he completely evaded any commitment to new gun laws. And Attorney General Mitchell, who swiftly endorsed wiretaps and mass police dragnets to preserve the peace, claims that after three years in office he needs "more study" on gun control. With this kind of hypocrisy, the Nixon administration is helping to sign the death warrants of more policemen.

TWO   Change police practices that hinder the work of deterrence

In many ways, the technical details of police practices, mandated by law, custom, or bureaucracy, cut down the efficiency of police; in some cases, police are actually deterred from making arrests.

A policeman who arrests a mugger may spend hours taking him to court for arraignment, waiting in court for a case to be called, writing out papers of the arrest. In most cities, a policeman making an arrest toward the end of his shift may spend extra hours taking the suspect through the initial stages of the criminal process with neither overtime pay nor extra time off. Even the most devoted cop is human; faced with the choice of wasted hours or a warm bed and food, he may well let a suspect go in those circumstances. Some police even find themselves spending two full shifts waiting for a traffic case to be called—while neighborhoods of high crime go without sufficient police protection.

The waste of police manpower—now the most costly local government service after education and welfare—is more harmful to public safety than a hundred Supreme Court decisions. Every police practice that wastes a cop's time in unnecessary rules should be junked. Sometimes this means simple procedural changes: assigning a few police to take a precinct's suspects to court at the same time, or substituting sworn depositions for the physical presence of an arresting officer at the arraignment stage, or summoning a policeman to traffic court only when the case is imminent.

And sometimes this means a fight against the police bureaucracy itself. In New York City, it took five years and a change in state law to let the city's police commissioner put more cops to work at night than in the morning—even though the crime rate was several times higher at night. And police unions in many areas will not let their men ride in one-man patrol cars—even though, in residential neighborhoods, this step could effectively double police presence, cutting down both on real crime and on the fear of citizens. It's boring and lonely working without a partner—but in this case at least, the interests of individual policemen are directly contrary to the job of stopping crime.

THREE Perhaps the most important step in fighting crime is to recognize that the criminal justice system is itself one of the great festering swamps of crime

When we think of our system of justice, we think of courts, the Constitution, the presumption of innocence, bail, and eloquent lawyers arguing for their clients' rights. But, as former New Haven Police Chief James Ahern has put it:

> That is not the law as it is experienced, the law as it happens every day. For most suspects—and judges and attorneys and policemen—the law is something much closer to . . . an ill-lit building, shabbily painted, where the plumbing does not work and the stairs are rickety. Instead of noble declarations, there is the mumble of a guilty plea—based on a hasty discussion between a criminal suspect and a lawyer he has probably never met and may never see again. Instead of the stately majesty of a trial, surrounded by the protection of eight centuries of tradition, there is a conference at the bench—the formal consummation of a private deal between a prosecutor and the defense counsel to reduce the charges against the suspect and move the calendar along.
>
> For such a suspect, his day in court is more likely a minute —or 45 seconds—because the judicial system is so crowded that there is no time to provide a trial for every suspect. And so an accused becomes, by his own admission, a convict; and he goes out of the courtroom, on his way to a so-called

correctional center. The odds are three to one he will return—accused of new offenses.

Thus, from the very beginning, a suspect is stripped of any connection with the community whose laws he has violated. He is isolated, turned into an object to be processed, driven further and further from any sense that he is a human being who matters. This kind of treatment is a catalyst of crime.

The same legislators and executives who are determined to "sweep the streets of crime" are those who vote against and block every attempt at making the criminal justice system effective at all: from judges who are picked for merit instead of political service, to an adequate staff of defense and prosecuting attorneys, everything that would really make the system work is opposed—because there is no constituency for change. It is always easy to economize when the victims are invisible. But the irony is, they are invisible only in a limited sense; for as long as we keep economizing this way, they will return as criminals, and as the creators of other victims.

FOUR   **The participation of the criminal's community—particularly for blacks, Chicanos, and Puerto Ricans—is important in breaking the crime cycle**

Today, a convict who has spent every day of his life in Hough or Watts or Harlem may find himself imprisoned hundreds of miles from his neighborhood, surrounded by guards, doctors, administrators, chaplains, and psychiatrists, all of whom are white and none of whom speak his language. It is inevitably an isolating experience. Experiments must be made to keep felons under custody in their own communities—using "halfway houses" and personnel who speak the language and reflect the culture of an inmate. However well-intentioned correctional officers may be, the ambience of a fortress under the control of another culture cripples the possibility of rehabilitation.

FIVE   The corruption of the criminal justice system— from the cop on the beat to judges on the bench and the politicians who pick them—is a direct cause of crime

The Knapp Commission hearings in New York City in the fall of 1971 disclosed what everyone already knew; that a pattern of corruption exists on the police force, which ranges from grocery store owners paying police to ignore Sabbath laws to systematic payments to police by large-scale prostitution, gambling, and narcotics operations.

Police corruption is a direct threat to crime-fighting. Apart from the obvious fact that criminals can avoid arrest (or can arrange arrests that are deliberately designed not to stand up in court) by paying off police, it feeds disrespect for the law. It is hard enough for, say, a white policeman to arrest a youthful black in a ghetto; if his victim has seen him shaking down a prostitute or ignoring the open sale of heroin, the sense of cynicism is likely to be complete.

But the issue of corruption is *not* limited to police; it is, in fact, a kind of elitism to fasten on the corruption of police —most of whom are from working-class backgrounds—while ignoring the corruption that infests the more "respectable" part of the criminal justice system. In many cities, judges pay set fees to political leaders for their judgeships; the ties between organized crime and established lawyers are often direct, and far more pervasive than the simple lawyer-client relationship. It is, moreover, sheer hypocrisy for Wall Street lawyers to put aside their tax-evasion schemes for a few months to moralize about police payoffs. Corruption is contagious, self-perpetuating, and damaging at any level. It cannot be wiped out of the police force while it is left to grow in other parts of the system of justice.

SIX   We have to understand the connection between our brutalizing prisons and our unsafe streets, and make prison reform the focus of any crusade against crime

Between 70 and 75 per cent of all crimes are committed by recidivists—by men and women who have been in jail before. The reason for this is simple: most inmates come out of jail more bitter, more turned against the straight world, than they were when they first entered jail. The term "corrections" is a hoax. Most penitentiaries are, in Ramsey Clark's phrase, "factories of crime."

Right now the corrections system is based on the concept of punishment rather than rehabilitation. It does not *say* that it is punishment-based; but the facts speak for themselves: of every federal dollar spent on corrections, 95 cents goes for pure custody purposes—bars, walls, guards; 5 cents goes for rehabilitation—job training and placement, education, medical care, better training for guards, work-release programs.

A basic change in the impulses of the corrections system is at the center of the new inmate "militancy"; if one actually reads the demands of the inmates of Attica, they seem modest, almost humble: a baseball field, more law books in the library, showers more than once a week, no censorship of mail and newspapers, removal of the screens between inmates and their families during visits so they might touch, better medical treatment, an end to custodial brutality, religious freedom, a minimum wage for work in the prison shop. These demands were mailed to the state commissioner of corrections *four months* before the rebellion that took forty-two lives broke out.

Only a month *before* Attica, a seventy-nine-page study released by a state senate committee warned conditions were so bad that future prison riots were inevitable. The report, prepared by Brooklyn State Senator Greenberg, said there were "no rehabilitation programs," not enough black and

Puerto Rican correction officers, "no full-time psychiatric services for inmates." It stated that "inmates were confined to their cells for excessive periods of time tantamount to cruel unusual punishment," and that "known narcotic addicts are being confined without any state treatment program." The Greenberg study argued that unless rehabilitation programs were started, "the expenditure of funds for arresting, prosecuting, and convicting is wasted. . . . To continue these conditions nullifies all other efforts at crime control."

Predictably, however, when Attica erupted, Governor Rockefeller was "shocked" and blamed the revolt on a conspiracy of a few incorrigible prisoners. And Spiro Agnew wrote in the *New York Times* that "our penal system remains among the most humane and advanced in the world."

Penologists, inmates, and prison reformers are almost unanimous about what needs to be done:

First, prison and court overcrowding could be alleviated by a more flexible attitude toward victimless crimes—gambling, prostitution, drunkenness, pot-smoking, homosexuality. These make up about half of the nontraffic arrests in the country. If the laws under which these arrests are made were eliminated, not only would it lessen overcrowding, but it would also permit police to focus on more serious crimes.

Second, prison rehabilitation programs should include: job training for jobs that actually exist on the outside; home furloughs for selected inmates as a deterrent to homosexuality and as a means of restoring an inmate's sense of bond with his community; permission for inmates to receive medical attention from their own doctors; repeal of all laws that prohibit the employment of exconvicts. (There are thirty-five different professions in New York State alone that bar exconvicts. Among them is barbering, a job for which many inmates are *trained* in prison.)

Third, a system of rewarding productive behavior should be included directly in the criminal justice system. The Vera Institute's Court Employment Project, begun as a small experiment in Manhattan in 1967, has become a great success. It provides jobs, group therapy, and a structured program for people awaiting trial. If participants get and hold a job and remain crime-free for three months, charges are dismissed by the court. The project now reaches forty people a week in New York City. It should be expanded and emulated by every jurisdiction.

Fourth, more professional parole boards that include psychiatrists and reformers who have direct contact with prisoners and a noncustodial bias (like Professor Herman Schwartz and Vera Director Herb Sturz) are needed. In too many places, parole boards are dumping grounds for patronage hacks with deep racial prejudices. In New York State, for example, parole board members serve six-year terms at $30,000 a year. Of the twelve current members, the youngest is fifty-one, although the overwhelming majority of inmates are under thirty-five. Ten members of the twelve are white, although seven of ten inmates are black or Puerto Rican. There is no woman on the board, although the crime rate among women is rising three times faster than among men.

Fifth, tear down every penitentiary built before 1900. These maximum-security zoos still exist in many states. (The Ohio Etate Penitentiary was built in *1834.*) They should be replaced by smaller jails of minimum and moderate security, so that inmates could be separated on the basis of age, seriousness of their offense, and their sexual predilections (the idea of homosexual jails is far less offensive than the reality of young men subject to rape and assault, often with the cooperation of prison guards).

SEVEN   **Something more than press agentry must be done about the heroin curse**

There are at least 300,000 addicts—perhaps as many as a million—living in the United States. Ten years ago, estimates ranged only up to 50,000, a number equaled today by the junkies in or back from Vietnam.

The "new Attorney General's" program to combat this horror seems to be nothing but a press-release campaign. In June of 1970, John Mitchell personally announced "the largest narcotics raid in history," and predicted that it would "diminish the flow of hard narcotics into the country."

In August of 1970, a federal prosecutor announced the smashing of "the largest ring ever uncovered in illegal narcotics traffic"; two months later, he boasted about the conviction of "the top importer of heroin into the United States."

In February of 1971, the Attorney General announced "the largest crackdown ever in narcotics distribution by organized crime."

In June of 1971, Mitchell said the Nixon administration "has mounted the most effective war on narcotics ever waged."

But in late July of 1971, a federal narcotics official told a congressional committee that, "heroin availability has not lessened . . . the purity of heroin is higher than ever . . . the price remains the same . . . and heroin-related deaths have increased." He concluded by saying, "the economy of heroin survives."

The heroin factor in crime is irrefutable. People steal to pay for their $50- and $100-a-day habits. More than 60 per cent of New York City's detention-jail inmates are junkies.

No single answer can stop heroin. Methadone—a substitute drug—works for some addicts; others respond better to therapeutic communities. More research funds are needed to test other chemical heroin substitutes—like the cyclazocine and naloxene some doctors believe can function as non-addictive drugs blocking the addict's euphoric "high." This may be one problem for which there is no reformist remedy.

In 1971, President Nixon requested $105 million for addict rehabilitation; compare that to his $290 million for the defeated SST, and the $250 million federally-guaranteed loan for Lockheed, and the sincerity of the President's commitment to "law and order" becomes perfectly clear. Until the national response to heroin addiction matches the depth of the epidemic, little will really be done to make the streets safe.

EIGHT   Increase citizen involvement in the police process

One way to prevent street crime is to encourage the formation of block and building associations to keep an eye on the streets and alleys, the hallways and elevators of the neighborhood. Police are not the only deterrent to street crime. The solidarity of neighbors, their willingness to protect each other, is effective in making streets safer.

We also think a policeman should live in or near the community he patrols. This proximity would improve the attitude of cop and citizen toward each other. It would also make civilian review of police power a realistic and feasible policy. Such a civilian watchdog agency, set up outside the police department, should have the power to investigate corruption and brutality as well as the invasion of privacy that results from electronic surveillance abuses.

11 ★ The Medical-Industrial Complex: Health

HEALTH CARE is a necessity. It should be a right. In America today, it is a luxury. The working poor can't afford doctors or hospitals, and every middle-class family knows that one serious illness can wipe out a lifetime's savings. Every big city has a segregated, two-class hospital system—private hospitals with modern technology and personalized care for the rich and insured, and understaffed municipal hospitals with beds in the halls and crowded wooden benches in the clinics for everyone else.

Medicare (for those over sixty-five) and Medicaid (for those earning less than $4,500 a year), after generating great hopes, have failed to effectively remedy the inequities. They haven't helped the almost-poor. The family that makes $6,000 a year is considered too affluent to qualify for Medicaid. But that same family can't afford private insurance, and is often not protected against long-term hospitalization and chronic illness. While Medicare and Medicaid have given health care to many people who could not previously have afforded it, these programs have also turned out to be windfalls for doctors and hospitals and a major cause of today's wildly escalating medical costs. Hospital bills have risen 125 per cent in ten years; doctor's fees have gone up by 150 per cent; and Blue Cross premium rates have increased almost every year during the past decade.

The average income for the nation's 335,000 licensed doctors is $40,500 a year; only 1 per cent of Americans earn as much. But black babies in the slums still die of undiagnosed lead poisoning and sickle-cell anemia. And, while pharmaceutical corporations like Pfizer and Eli Lilly are making all-time record profits, lots of elderly citizens can't afford the inflated prices of prescription medicines.

There are publicized heart transplants and prestigious open heart surgery units in Houston's glittering medical complex. But Puerto Ricans still bleed to death in the dingy emergency waiting room of Lincoln Hospital in the South Bronx.

The United States is ahead of the rest of the world in medical technology and research. But America ranks fourteenth among industrial nations of the world in infant mortality rates, twelfth in maternal mortality, eighteenth in male life expectancy at birth, and eleventh for women.

In 1970, a nonpresidential year, the AMA contributed $700,000 to candidates opposed to national health insurance. But there are unhealthy children in Appalachia who haven't seen a doctor since they were born.

One simple syllogism seems to sum up health care in America. The poor get sick. The sick get poor. And the medical-industrial complex gets richer all the time.

Escalating costs is the most obvious failure of the American medical system.

In August of 1969, John DeLury, the colorful leader of New York City's Sanitationmen's Union, testified before the Public Service Commission against a rate increase requested by Blue Cross. He told this story about the son of a member of his union:

A ten-year-old boy was admitted to a hospital at 3:20 a.m. The boy died at 10:34 the same night. The family of this child was charged $105.80 for drugs; $184.80 for X-rays; $220.00 for inhalation therapy; $655.50 for laboratory work. The hospital bill for the dead child was $1,717.80, or $86.73 per hour of hospitalization.

In the spring of 1971, Senator Ted Kennedy's health subcommittee held a public hearing in the heart of Appalachia, in Kingwood, West Virginia. In one afternoon, the press heard three elderly men describe how they couldn't pay for the medicines needed to heal them, and listened to a weeping Mrs. Delores Kempher talk about the illnesses of her five children and her inability to get treatment for them because she was "too rich" for Medicaid.

After the hearing, Kennedy led the press down an unpaved back road near an abandoned coal mine to the crumbling shack where Mrs. Edna Moats lived with her three children. (Her husband had died of black lung eight years before.) One of the Moats children, Cecil, was mentally retarded, and played in the junk-filled yard making animal noises. A second child was grossly obese with what seemed to be a thyroid condition. Mrs. Moats explained to the Senator that neither child had seen a doctor in years because she "couldn't afford it."

In one Boston hospital, a bed in the intensive care unit for respiratory diseases now costs *$425.75 per day*. In the last two years, Blue Cross has been awarded rate increases of 43 per cent in New York, 25 per cent in Connecticut, 44 per cent in New Jersey, 33 per cent in Rhode Island. A study prepared by statistical experts in the Social Security Administration has predicated that medical expenses will rise 50 per cent by 1975, that the average family will pay an additional *$200 a year* in medical bills by the middle of the decade.

The same study projected a 13 per cent increase in hospital costs *every year*.

We believe the primary reason for these outrageous costs is that the institutions currently in control of health care are motivated by greed: Blue Cross and other insurance outfits, the international drug companies, and the AMA.* Only when health care is perceived as a basic right like education, and not as a scarce commodity to be sold at a profit, will this situation be improved.

Three-quarters of all hospital bills are paid through the mechanism of Blue Cross. There are more than seventy separate municipal, regional, and state-wide Blue Cross plans in the country. They are all tax-exempt and, in theory, regulated by state insurance boards.

Given its extensiveness, Blue Cross is in a key position to determine health care costs—and to hold them down. But Blue Cross has abdicated this power. It has, in fact, by its own acts and by its policies, helped increase costs for the average citizen.

First, it has constantly kept increasing its own rate premiums. Rarely have the state regulatory boards denied Blue Cross its increases. And second, Blue Cross pays hospitals on a costs-plus basis. Hospitals just say how much they need to cover costs and Blue Cross pays it without checking. There have been differences of 100 per cent between two hospitals for identical services. These costs are passed on to subscribers in the form of rate increases. In practice, Blue Cross subscribers are also unwittingly paying for hospital lawyers and public relations staffs who battle against unionization of low-paid hospital workers. They also pay for consultants, empty beds, and expensive technologies that serve only a few patients.†

* We do not primarily blame the individual doctor. He is no more responsible for the whole system than the individual cop is responsible for the condition of the courts and jails.

† A congressional committee recently discovered that one local plan was paying the country club dues of Blue Cross executives. (*New York Times*, September 13, 1971.)

Blue Cross is dominated by the hospital establishment, which created it to make sure bills were paid. The trademark "Blue Cross" is owned by the American Hospitals Association. Blue Cross subscribers are not stockholders, and have no say how the plan is managed. The typical Blue Cross plan provides for a self-recruited board of trustees. Nowhere in the country do subscribers have a voice in choosing the trustees. Most subscribers are not even sure what their policy covers until after they get sick.

Until recently, Blue Cross units dominated the state agencies that were supposed to regulate them. For example, Thomas Thatcher was New York State's Superintendent of Insurance from 1959 until 1963. During that time, he granted Blue Cross several substantial rate increases. Today Thatcher is a member of the board of New York Blue Cross.

But in 1970, several Governors finally appointed reformers who were actually willing to regulate Blue Cross. Dr. Herbert Denenberg is the new insurance commissioner in Pennsylvania. One of his first decisions was to reject a $74 million premium rate increase sought by Philadelphia Blue Cross, which had been granted a rate hike for each of the twenty-five preceding years.

Another cost problem for the health consumer is that Blue Cross offers the least protection for the most common situations—maternity, dental care, and nursing homes. Its most common coverage is surgeon's fees, which may be the reason, critics believe, many unnecessary operations are being performed. In fact, most insurance policies have no incentive toward ambulatory or preventive care, which is, of course, cheaper than hospitalization and surgery.

Blue Cross is the most extensive of the operators in the health-insurance business, and in this way it sets the pace. But, as too many privately insured Americans have discovered, the other companies engage in practices that border on the criminal. The fifty-seven-year-old man who, having suffered his first heart attack, finds his health insurance canceled—after having paid premiums for perhaps twenty years —is not alone. And the premiums go up—along with health-care costs—for all Americans.

If the insurance companies, led by Blue Cross, are major contributors to this health-care cost inflation, the drug companies are right in step. The May, 1971 issue of *Fortune* contained its annual accounting of corporate gains and losses. And despite the national recession and a shaky stock market, the drug companies were doing very well. In rating different industries on their return on total capital, pharmaceuticals ranked first, ahead of tobacco, mining, and other profitable businesses. Two of the ten most profitable corporations for stockholders manufactured drugs—Merck, and Smith, Kline and French. Of the ten corporations with the biggest increase in sales for the previous year, one manufactured drugs (Warner-Lambert). Prescription drugs are a $2 billion-a-year business—and $800 million of that just goes for public relations and advertising.

A lot of that profit comes from exaggerated prices, negotiated monopolies on drug patents, worthless patent medicine, and manipulated fears created and heightened by slick advertising. Fifteen years ago, Senator Kefauver exposed the tricks the big drug companies use to mulct the sick and the old. Most brand-name prescription drugs (e.g., Librium) cost five and ten times more than if customers asked for them under their generic name ("cloridizapoxide"). Few doctors, however, write generic-name prescriptions—and the drug companies bombard them with ads, brochures, samples, and other items intended to keep the brand name on the prescription pads. Harry Simmons, chief drug officer of the Food and Drug Administration, estimates that Americans spend half a billion dollars every year on useless drugs. Congressional investigations have shown some pharmaceutical companies have made as much as 1000 per cent profits on some specific drugs. And these profits are made without real competition, since a handful of corporations dominate this most profitable of all industries; there are 700 drug firms in the country, but the top 15 sell more than half the drugs.

The third member in this health-care troika is the AMA. Although its power now appears somewhat diminished, the AMA has been a well-financed, well-organized lobby against better medical care since the 1930's. (It was founded in 1847, but did not turn political until the New Deal.)

In his brilliant book *A Sacred Trust,* Richard Harris chronicled the AMA's forty-year campaign against Medicare, which it characterized as "socialized medicine" and "a step toward communism." Today, the AMA helps keep costs high by limiting the size of medical school classes, and thus keeping the supply of doctors below the demand.* It has also failed to support any effort to bring down the costs of trade name prescription drugs, perhaps because so much of the AMA's income is drawn from the ads in its journal that are taken by pharmaceutical companies.

Two recent episodes provide a glimpse of how this professional association of physicians intervenes in the political process.

In January of 1970, then-HEW Secretary Robert Finch declared his intention of selecting Dr. John Knowles, the liberal head of the Massachusetts General Hospital, as his Assistant Secretary for Health. The AMA objected, preferring a more conservative nominee, and set to work to block Knowles.

Its principal tool in this fight was the medical profession's political arm—the American Medical Political Action Committee (AMPAC)—set up in 1965 after the passage of

* In 1934, AMA President, Dr. Walter L. Biering, said "One is forced to the conviction that more doctors are being turned out than society needs and can comfortably reward . . . a fine piece of educational work could well be done if we were to use only half of the seventy-odd medical schools in the United States." Faced with this pressure, medical schools sharply cut back enrollments—only in 1958 did the AMA begin to acknowledge that there was a "critical shortage" of doctors.

Medicare and primarily intended to serve as an agency to distribute campaign contributions to conservative politicians. When the Knowles appointment became known, AMPAC was cranked up for an all-out lobbying effort.

In 1968 AMPAC had disbursed $700,000, which might explain why Congressman Bob Wilson, chairman of the Republican Congressional Campaign Committee, quickly agreed to oppose the Knowles appointment. So did the late Everett Dirksen, then Republican Minority Leader in the Senate, and traditionally an AMA advocate. The AMA also convinced Representative Rogers Morton, then GOP National Chairman, that the Knowles appointment would mean less money to local candidates in 1970. So on June 26, Secretary Finch withdrew his sponsorship of Dr. Knowles.*

The second episode surfaced in July of 1971, when Senator Ted Kennedy opened a public hearing into the fate of four reports drafted by four Presidential Commissions (Katzenbach, Kerner, Scranton, and Eisenhower), each containing a statement attacking the AMA's historic opposition to new health legislation.

A few days later, the Democratic Senatorial Campaign Committee received a letter from Harry Hinton, the AMA's chief lobbyist, warning that AMPAC would stop all contributions to Democrats throughout the country if Kennedy's criticism did not end. "The AMA will get every physician in the country to leave the Democratic Party," Hinton's letter warned. Kennedy called it "the most candid document he had ever seen," and read the whole letter into the *Congressional Record* (July 22, 1971, S. 11721).

In addition to these three institutions, a fourth is currently preventing more and better health care—the Nixon administration.

Although the President signed the Emergency Health Personnel Act of 1970, which permits health professionals to do

* The AMA, however, could not stop Finch from naming another liberal—Dr. Roger Egeberg—to the same post.

alternative draft service by practicing medicine in regions where there is a shortage of doctors, the law has never been implemented. The President also signed the Ryan-Kennedy bill, which authorized $30 million over two years to test for and treat lead poisoning. Yet, though it was enacted late in 1970, not one dollar has actually been spent. Congress authorized $75 million for preventive programs to vaccinate children against rubella, diptheria, and other diseases, but less than $2 million has actually been used by the executive agencies involved in the program. The President has vetoed three bills providing federal fund for health programs, all after he officially pronounced a "massive crisis" in medical care in July of 1969.

On July 27, 1971, liberals in the House submitted an amendment to the HEW appropriation bill that would have added $230 million to the budget, largely for preventive health programs. The amendment included funding for diagnosis and treatment of alcoholism, lead poisoning, environmental diseases (like black lung), and venereal disease, as well as funding for mental health centers and narcotics addiction rehabilitation programs. White House and HEW staff members lobbied furiously by memo and telephone against the amendment. In the end, it was defeated, 215 to 169,* and noticed in only a few lines of type the next morning in the *New York Times*. But for those of us who remembered John Mitchell's injunction—"Please judge us by what we do, not what we say"—it was an instructive day to be sitting in the press gallery.

Major changes in approach as well as in programs are needed to reform the present health-care system. We argue for the following:

* Among those who voted against the health amendment were the misnamed "last populist" Wright Patman, and this year's Gene McCarthy—Pete McCloskey.

ONE **A free and decentralized system that treats rich and poor equally should be our national policy**

We must accept the essential concept of health care as a public service like education, to be paid for by an equitable tax system. It has taken thirty-five years to get national health insurance onto the practical political agenda. We must now be prepared for another generation-long struggle to enact universal public health care based on the successful Swedish and British models. We can begin by frankly stating that as our goal.

TWO **The immediate political issue now before the nation is some form of national health insurance**

If universal public health care is our long-term objective, national health insurance is an immediate possibility. At least fifty different bills have been introduced in the last sessions of Congress proposing some form of NHI. Most of these bills represent the worst sort of political cynicism. Congressmen and senators have been lining up to get their names on any kind of bill that will prove to their constituents they are in favor of universal health care. But most of these bills will never even be the subject of a public hearing, much less a floor vote. Most have been filed and forgotten just as soon as the initial press release was in the mail to the home-town papers. And most are essentially conceived to please the AMA or Blue Cross, making no real effort to better the quality of patient care or to improve the delivery of health services.

The administration's plan—the National Health Insurance Partnership Act—would tax the poor to provide a windfall for the insurance industry. The AMA's own plan—Medicredit—is bereft of cost or quality controls. A "compromise" plan put forth by Senator Javits—the National Health Insurance and Health Services Improvement Act—leaves out many needed benefits for the poor and contains few incentives to better case.

The only barely adequate, although hardly sufficient, plan as yet introduced is that put forward by Senator Kennedy. It is based on the original proposal drafted by the late Walter Reuther and the Committee of 100. Kennedy's legislation— the Health Security Act—offers "cradle to grave" nationalized insurance for every citizen. Benefits would include hospitalization and home nursing care; dental and eye care; prescription drugs; the costs of all surgery; and most private psychiatric care. General tax revenues would provide 50 per cent of the cost, with the other half coming from a 3 per cent payroll tax on employers and a 1 per cent payroll tax on employees.

The Reuther-Kennedy plan also includes economic incentives to reform the entire health system. It encourages group practice, health maintenance organizations, rural location of doctors, controls on drug prescribing, and systematic hospital planning.

National health insurance was first seriously proposed by Franklin Roosevelt in 1935; it was raised next by Senator Robert Wagner, Sr. in 1943, and again, by Harry Truman in January of 1948. Each time, the AMA mobilized its forces and managed to kill the idea. Now that it seems to be an idea whose time has finally come, the cynics are trying to confuse the public by sponsoring so many counterfeits that no one can get the different versions sorted out. But, contrary to what some radicals say, we think the fight to pass the Reuther-Kennedy plan is not a meaningless diversion. It deserves the strongest possible support. It will help the blue-collar and middle-class family to receive better medical care —and it will help them now. But it will not restructure the private health system or take the corporate profits out of it. That is another, more long-range fight.

THREE   Private institutions must be reformed if there is to be better care at lower costs

If public health care is not merely to become private wealth for insurance companies, a system of review and regulation must be put into effect. This means consumer representation on regulatory agencies. It may mean government operations to provide a yardstick on costs. It means strict supervision and periodic checks on hospital costs. And doctors' fees. But it also means taking the exorbitant profits out of the drug industry—not only by encouraging the use of generic prescribing but also by reviews of monopoly patents where called for.

FOUR   **Preventive medicine must become a higher priority for the entire profession**

Everything from free vaccination programs and school lunches to research into the causes and treatment of alcoholism and drug addiction comes under the heading of preventive medicine. The TB mobile testing unit on the ghetto street and the comprehensive diagnostic bus in the rural county are part of the same concept of preventive medical care. So too are rat control, prenatal care, local clinic services, screening programs for sickle-cell anemia and lead poisoning, and decent salaries for public health doctors, nurses, and paraprofessionals. These things are obvious. What is less clearly understood but equally important is how the kind of medical research undertaken in this country today affects preventive medicine. Profit motivates research done by pharmaceutical firms, so that all their work is drug-related; but profit need not and should not motivate government-funded efforts to find the causes for existing diseases. Right now, more money—public as well as private—is channeled into finding cures rather than determining causes or diagnostic methods to track a disease before it becomes incurable. It was in England, not the United States, that the PAP-smear to detect cervical cancer was developed and made freely and easily available to all women, regardless of income. This is the kind of preventive medicine that a country as wealthy as America should be doing.

FIVE   **The routes into the medical profession must be opened up to minorities, and to those whose skills can help save lives even without the full training necessary to become a doctor of medicine**

One of the classic rationalizations for the high incomes of doctors is that the training to become a doctor is expensive, specialized, and prolonged. Certainly the ten years from the start of college to the end of internship is lengthy and expensive; but in addition to producing a sense among some doctors that this gives them the right to earn what the traffic will bear, it ensures a choice between an inadequate number of doctors and an enormously expensive process of "catch-up" medical education.

There *is* an alternative: and that is the introduction into medicine of great numbers of people with limited but useful skills, people who can both save lives and the time of doctors and relieve the crushing burden of costs.

There is room in medicine for those of every level of skills. No one suggests that a "hard-core" unemployed trainee be permitted to dabble in open-heart surgery. But we have already found, for example, that "paraprofessionals" can be used for a number of tasks, ranging from feeding and caring for patients to the routine work of checking medical supplies. Medical technicians can be trained in a year or two to operate machinery and take tests on patients that free doctors for more demanding tasks.

But what must now be recognized—despite the ingrained thinking which holds that only traditionally trained doctors can be entrusted with the health of a patient—is that alternate routes to medical proficiency exist and can be used to save lives and money. For example, in Vietnam, medics undergo a twelve-week training program, on the basis of which they have saved lives on the battlefield. They do not have medical degrees or even college educations; but they do have the skill to turn a helicopter into a life-saving ambulance. Their skill is the principal reason that the death rate from Vietnam combat wounds is the lowest of any war in history.

To bring these trained medics back to the States and then to let them look for jobs as welders or cabdrivers is sheer waste. This talent could be put into the emergency rooms of municipal hospitals all over America to save the lives of auto accident victims and other critically ill patients. They could help staff health facilities in Appalachia, or other rural areas where the shortage of doctors is endemic. Indeed, they could even be encouraged, through loans and income supplements, to become doctors by attending classes while working in hospitals.

This kind of thinking may be one way of bringing new and needed medical care to Americans who now lack it.

SIX Consumer and community participation (not control) must become part of the running of local health centers

If a level of trust and cooperation is to be established between the public and the professionals, the public must be brought into the health business. For too long, health administrators and doctors have spoken in their exclusive professional jargon; for too long they have ignored the public they serve. Instead, we propose that hospitals and other medical services institutions be run by elected boards consisting of staff and community representatives, which would replace existing boards now dominated by bankers and philanthropists.

12 ★ Labor Pains: Unions and Work

DUFFY RAINES started working in the coal mines of Appalachia when he was thirteen years old. Now, in his late sixties, he is forced to work as a watchman for $75 a month and a ramshackle trailer for his shelter. The United Mine Workers, after collecting his dues for thirty-one years, refuses to give him his $115-a-month pension—and the UMW retirement fund won't give Duffy Raines a hearing on his case.

The biggest construction employer in New York State is the state government, now building such enormous projects as the billion-dollar Albany Mall. State law requires that preference for state construction jobs be given to New York residents. Yet, despite the presence of thousands of qualified, unemployed New York skilled workers, more than $150 million worth of state funds goes to out-of-state workers; more than 30,000 of them work on public projects. In one New York City local, 42 per cent of the membership comes from outside the greater New York area, from as far away as Ohio and Tennessee. In the Buffalo area, 15 per cent of all new construction jobs have gone to Canadians. Why? The New Yorkers are black and Puerto Rican—and the New York labor locals don't want to admit them to membership.

In the auto plants of Michigan, absenteeism is running at record rates—on Mondays and Fridays, it runs as high as 20 per cent, and cars made on these weekend-bordering days are substantially worse in quality than those made on other days. Shop stewards report an alarming rise in drug use by younger workers; some of whom sneak into washrooms to use pot, speed, and even heroin.

After the leaders of the New York taxidrivers' union pushed through a 50 per cent fare increase, drivers found their incomes actually reduced. Fewer riders were taking cabs, and tips were way down. The cab owners, and those drivers who owned their own cabs, were doing better, but the average hack was in trouble. A group of dissidents demanded a union meeting to air their grievances; those who rose to speak were physically attacked, beaten, and thrown out of the hall.

These illustrations point out different kinds of trouble in the ranks of labor. But the common thread linking them is that the interests of workers and the interests of labor unions and leaders are not always the same. Sometimes this gap has grown because of outright greed and venality on the part of some union chiefs. More often, however, the problem is more basic: labor organizations, which fought hard and well for the rights of their members forty and fifty years ago, have continued to fight the old battles while new issues—new grievances on the part of working Americans—have gone almost unheeded. We do not accept in any sense the proposition that the labor movement is obsolete or irrelevant. The effort to redistribute wealth and power cannot succeed without unions.

Moreover, we recognize that labor was one of the institutions that tried to keep many basic issues of economic justice alive during the 1950's and 1960's, when more affluent liberals were abandoning them. While Daniel Bell and Arthur Schlesinger argued that the basic questions of poverty and wealth had been resolved, some key unions were struggling for national health insurance, federal aid to education, and tax reform.

But we do believe that unions have tended to follow the example of corporate power too often; they have been trapped into identifying their interests narrowly, shielding what power they have won instead of sharing it with their natural allies. In some fields, such as racial justice and foreign policy, substantial segments of the union movement in America have aligned themselves with the most reactionary forces in American life. And, by equating *jobs* with their interests, at the cost of every other concern, they have actually hurt the men and women of labor.

At times, parts of American labor have behaved just as their bosses; indeed, watching labor and management is sometimes like watching the men and the pigs in Orwell's animal farm—you can't tell one from the other. No American capitalist looks or acts the part more than George Meany, even to the chauffered limousine and cigar. But the real injuries to American workers from their ostensible "protectors" go substantially beyond image.

Take the case of the United Mine Workers, led for decades by John L. Lewis, one of the towering figures and imposing voices of the rights of workers. Sadly, Lewis's legacy is a shabby remnant of his rhetorical promises. The Mine Workers' retirement fund was supposed to give men who had risked their lives every day in the coal mines of Kentucky and West Virginia some security when they grew too old to work. Instead, the pension fund was used to enrich the union and its top officials. More than $67 million was kept in an interest-free account at the National Bank of Washington, at a loss of $3 million a year in interest. This practice enriched the bank—and the UMW, which owned 73 per cent of the bank's stock. But it bled the pension fund dry.

To prevent the retirement fund from going bankrupt, the Mine Workers began denying pensions to miners who had spent their lives in the mines. Men like Duffy Raines. And Howard Linville—who has a birth certificate proving he was born in 1911, but who the union says was born in 1914, making him too young to qualify. The retirement board won't credit miners with time on the picket lines, or time spent looking for jobs, even if these men kept their dues up: because giving pensions to all the men who earned them would have exposed the mismangement of the fund.

Interestingly, when it came to protecting the pensions of union officers, the UMW was more solicitous. For union officers, its pension fund was scrupulously managed by experts, enabling officials to retire at full pay—up to $50,000 a year for UMW President Tony Boyle. (The average miner retires on about $1,380 a year—when he can get it.)

When Boyle was challenged for the union presidency by Joseph Yablonski, hundreds of charges of unfair practices were filed against the UMW—but Nixon's Labor Secretary George Shultz refused to move, and AFL-CIO President Meany said, "it was just that one of the boys from the kitchen is trying to move into the living room." Shortly after the disputed election, Yablonski, his wife, and his daughter were murdered, and the dispute turned into a public scandal that could no longer be ignored. Boyle is now under indictment for misusing UMW pension funds.

In the late 1950's, many trade unionists and their supporters said that investigations against unions were promoted by business interests seeking to discredit labor. Some civil libertarians protested against the congressional committee tactics—and later, the Justice Department tactics—or Robert Kennedy. But the point most often overlooked was that the dishonest practices of the UMW, the Teamsters, and other like unions *hurt the interests of the workers.* To enrich them-selves, union leaders jeopardized the pensions of their work-ers, and, on occasion, sold out their interests through "sweet-heart" contracts with employers.

Similarly, the reporting and disclosure requirements of the Landrum-Griffin Act *did* have a basis in justice: in many cases, union leaders elected themselves virtually in secret, much as a corporate board of directors might. Dissident union officials found themselves, as in the National Maritime Union and New York's UFT, suddenly fired from their jobs.

The automatic objections labor raises when confronted by federal laws like the Landrum-Griffin Act indicate the under-lying, fundamental difficulty with much of the labor move-ment today: *the identification of their interests in the nar-rowest possible terms.* More than any specific reform or leg-islation, a change in this attitude is vital to the building of a new alliance for economic and social justice.

Murray Kempton once said of the construction unions, "they would build gas ovens if it was steady work." Without going that far, it is unquestionable that in almost every case in recent history, labor has supported any expenditure of funds, no matter how dangerous or wasteful, if it put union members to work. Labor has always been one of the strong voices in Congress for new weapons systems; it lobbied hard for the SST and the Lockheed loan; it has urged continuation of the Highway Trust Fund. With the single exception of Walter Reuther's opposition to the antiballistic missile— which West Coast UAW members would help build—labor has never said "the money is needed for other projects." Its attitude has been, "what's good for this union is good for America." It is a short-range view.

Labor unions have also consistently sought to cut off the supply of labor; to limit the number of those entitled to work in a field. The reason is simple: the lower the supply, the more the cost of labor is driven up. Just as doctors suc-ceeded forty years ago in cutting medical school enrollments and driving up medical fees, the craft unions—plumbers, electricans, sheet-metal workers, iron mongers—have opposed all suggestions for opening up their ranks, not just to black and Puerto Rican members, but to all but a handful of new card holders and these are often the relatives of presently enrolled journeymen.

For the same reason, labor has joined hands with management to embrace protectionist policies toward imports. U.S. Steel and the steelworkers want quotas on foreign steel; the textile workers and their employers stand together in opposition to free imports.

Work rules—most notably in railroads and printing—have also helped to keep costs high at the price of improved productivity. We can't build housing for less than $35,000 a unit in New York, even though the technology to build low-income, prefabricated housing with prefab plumbing units has existed for years. Railroad unions still won't let new technology into the driver's seat, and printers still set "dead horse"—setting in type printed matter already molded into plastic forms. (The "dead horse" is thrown away. Newspapers fold because they can't afford the costs, and the same unions that imposed archaic work rules to protect their members now find hundreds of them out of work.)

The irony is that these kinds of efforts to hold on to the small share of economic power that labor has are often self-defeating. For example, since World War II American railroads have eliminated 1.1 million jobs; the rise in housing costs have brought low- and middle-income housing to a standstill in America, wiping out the possibility of tens of thousands of jobs.

And the embrace of protectionism threatens as many jobs as it may save. Apart from the disastrous consequences of the 1920's trade wars between America and Europe, the nations that labor fears provide almost as many jobs as they threaten. For example, Japan has increased American jobs by importing from us six times as much coal—$412 million worth

—in 1970 as it did it in 1966. More than 75 per cent of wheat grown by the state of Washington's farmers went to Japan. And a University of Wisconsin study revealed that if the protectionist walls went up between America and Japan, the United States would lose six high-paying jobs for every seven jobs it "protected."

Ironically, the passionate fights of many craft unions to "protect" their members from other men who seek jobs has not extended to protecting their health and safety. Despite all of the industrial safety legislation, 14,000 American workers die on the job every year and more than 2 million are sickened or maimed. Yet construction unions have never made safety a major bargaining issue. For years, skyscrapers in big cities were built using asbestos spray to fireproof the structure; union leaders never bothered to find out that asbestos, taken into the lungs, was linked with cancer, pneumoconeosis, and other lung diseases. These union leaders knew how to bargain for extra sick days or more medical insurance, but the idea that the health of their members might be a legitimate bargaining issue in itself—that, for example, unions might demand safe substances on the job— rarely occurred to the craft unions. Similar indifference was found in the mines, where it took a wildcat strike to get a "black lung" law through Congress. The Mine Workers, with financial interests in the mines, turned its back on its own members.

Except for its embrace of rigid, at times hysterical, anti-communism as a foreign policy, nothing has tainted the American labor movement more than a continuing stain of racism. From the efforts of Samuel Gompers to impose restrictive immigration laws to the court fights by craft unions against government programs to hire minority workers, racial discrimination has been with labor for too much of its history. While this bias is partially linked to the broader issue of keeping the labor supply small, it has been a disservice to a movement claiming to stand for social justice.

The racial issue is going to grow in importance to labor, especially in the semiskilled jobs, where many of the new workers are blacks, Puerto Ricans, and other minorities. While organized labor in the semiskilled sector has not fought to keep minorities out—for one thing, there's nowhere else to turn for new labor in these fields—it has fought efforts at bringing minorities into positions of leadership within the unions. New York's ILGWU (International Ladies' Garment Workers Union), a bastion of democratic socialist thought a generation ago and a catalyst in the founding of the Liberal Party, is now heavily made up of blacks and Puerto Ricans. But the executive leadership remains overwhelmingly white; significantly, in 1969 the ILGWU worked hard for the most reactionary of the candidates for mayor of New York.

This pattern of white leadership and minority-group membership extends elsewhere. More than half of Chicago's transit workers are blacks; but the union leadership is almost all white. To perpetuate this rule, the Transit Union allows retired workers—who are 99 per cent white—to vote in union elections.

The pattern is not inevitable. In New York City, three of the most progressive unions—Local 1199, Hospital Workers; District 65, Retail Clerks; and District 37, American Federation of State, County, and Municipal Employees—have all democratized their leadership to permit participation by racial minorities. But the general pattern remains unyielding; nothing can be more dangerous to the already fragile coalition of blacks and working-class white than this kind of division within the ranks of labor.

Perhaps the most difficult dilemmas faced by labor unions are those that surround the whole question of work. The United Auto Workers, for example, has been one of the best unions in America; fighting for racial justice, opposing the cold war mentality of George Meany and Jay Lovestone, raising issues like national health insurance and the guaranteed annual wage in advance of every other union.

Yet now the UAW finds itself faced with the question of the work on the auto lines in and of itself; it finds that more and more of its younger members simply do not want to spend thirty or forty years doing the same mechanical work eight hours of every working day of their lives.

Fifteen years ago, writer Frank Marquat described life in the auto factory:

> Not only does the factory look like a prison from the outside, but it also has a prison-like regimen. There are the uniformed plant guards stationed at the gate . . . there are strict shop rules and regulations and there are the "plant protection police" to see that the rules are observed; there is the factory routine and discipline . . . workers must punch in their time cards, stay in prescribed areas in the shop, take their places at the assembly line or machine, and then work under compulsions exacted by the mass production process.

Thirty-five years ago, with a steady job as the goal, that kind of life might be looked on as rewarding—at least, compared to enforced idleness and poverty. Today, however, in the midst of a cultural revolution that has touched every part of American life, the idea of spending a lifetime working, eating, resting, and moving at the commands of a machine or a superior looks something like slavery; even if the wages are good, the *life* is not. And when we add to this the fact that a man who seeks to leave his job may have to wait twenty or thirty years before having the right to any part of his pension, the life of even a well-paid skilled worker looks like something close to indentured servitude.

The issue here, then, goes to a union's concern with the worker *as a human being*—with making his work rewarding, and even making it possible for him to change jobs or seek news kinds of work. We have almost never regarded such issues—beyond the basic areas of working conditions, time off, and retirement rights—as "labor" isues. But the way a worker spends his life, the opportunity he has to seek new work, is as important a question as the traditional rights of collective bargaining.

For a twenty-year-old of the middle class, regimentation is almost nonexistent. If he is in college, he can cut classes to read, or relax, or get stoned. If he wants to hitchhike across America, all he needs is a thumb and a knapsack. If he wants to go to Europe the airlines will fly him there for half-fare. The idea that someone could tell him when he can eat, when he can go to the bathroom, how he must move for a third of his life, would be a black comic fantasy. For his counterpart in the work force, however, it is a reality. For the young worker, the trip to Europe will be on a military transport— because there is no 2-S deferment for people who work with their hands. There is virtually no way that such a man will ever do anything different than what he does on that first morning he walks into a factory.

This is very much a populist issue because it deals with the power of men and women over their own lives. The enormous gulf in autonomy is one of the hidden issues in America. It accounts in part for the rage workers feel when they see students striking against universities or dressing androgynously, for such actions and dress suggest that these cultural dissidents have escaped from the rigors of a mechanized, alienated life.

We do not believe that any political step can fully resolve the basic questions of work and labor in America. But a series of steps can make labor a full partner in the work of economic and social justice.

ONE **Craft unions should adopt flexible rules for badly-needed construction**

Pete Hamill has noted that theatrical unions charge lower rates and adopt more flexible rules for low-budget and off-Broadway productions. If craft unions did the same for needed housing, it would bring the cost down substantially and make investment more attractive. These funds would, in turn, open up more jobs than existing craft union members could possibly fill. Coupled with stringent enforcement of antidiscrimination laws, such new jobs would mean work for thousands of minority group members now frozen out of the job market.

TWO   Join the effort to find new technology

If we can build housing for poor and working people with prefabricated methods, plastic prefitted pipes, and other techniques, it is ultimately self-defeating for labor unions to fight these steps. There is no reason why union members would not find well-paid jobs if new technology made it possible to build rapid-transit systems, pollution control devices, and housing for less cost. In any event, we believe that political figures have to bite the bullet on this issue. Permitting unions to stop needed projects and inflate costs is as unfair a use of economic power as the administered prices of corporations and the exorbitant profiteering of banks and insurance companies.

THREE   Make pension funds fully "portable"

There is no reason why a worker who has put in a reasonable amount of time in a job—say, five years—should have to feel chained to that one job because his pension rights do not "vest" for twenty or thirty years. If a worker has earned pension money, and wants to try his luck at another job or strike out on his own, the pension funds he has earned should be available to him. Better still, they should be transferable at full equity.

FOUR Use union resources to enable workers to train for new careers

A thirty-year-old assembly line worker with a family and a mortgage is effectively chained to his job for life. Even if he has the talent and the inclination to go to college or technical school, he cannot support his family while trying for a different life.

Unions now have more than $60 billion in pension funds, largely invested by banks and insurance companies. If a small fraction of that money was made available for loans to workers seeking new careers, it would open up autonomy for men and women now trapped in one boring job for life. Government could insure these loans, much as it insures bank deposits and mortgage loans—the cost to taxpayers would be minimal. This proposal was suggested almost six years ago by Adam Walinsky, but it has gone unnoticed. It is time that union leadership began to face up to the question of individual autonomy and the lack of opportunity union members now have to exercise that autonomy.

FIVE Expand union participation in management

Yugoslavia is one of the few communist nations actually experimenting with worker participation in management decisions. Through workers' councils, the men and women who manufacture the product have a say in the day-to-day operations of a factory or plant. This goal should be an urgent priority matter for labor now.

For example, unions ought to begin making membership on the company's board of directors a bargaining issue. (The purchase of a token share of company stock would satisfy any legal requirement that directors come from the ranks of shareholders.) It would be interesting to see whether management could ignore issues like pollution and worker safety if men and women who actually knew the daily functioning of an industry had a voice on the board of directors. It might also result in efforts to free work patterns from the debilitating, mechanistic style that now drains the spirit of so many workers.

SIX Organize the unorganized—southerners, the young, blacks, women, clerical workers, farm laborers

Less than 18 per cent of the labor force is organized and the vast pool of those who are unorganized affects the bargaining power of those who are in unions. Garment workers in New York are still exploited, sometimes earning less than the legal minimum wage, because the South remains a low-wage haven, unorganized by unions.

Except for the hospital workers and the farm workers, no new organizing is being done. Labor's first priority should be a massive drive to unionize millions of workers. This would not only create national wage standards, but would also help generate the thrust from below that is critical if the old and stale leadership of many international unions is to be moved out.

13 ★ Fight Fiercely, Harvard: Foreign Policy

THE SONS of Harvard and Yale sent the sons of Watts and South Boston to die in Vietnam.

That is a harsh view of foreign policy. But it is true. For decades, the essential decisions affecting American foreign policy have been made by the American elite: by men (women have been almost totally excluded from this process) who brought with them the perceptions and judgments of the most privileged American institutions. John Foster Dulles, the apologist for fascism in the '30's and the xenophobic anticommunist of the '50's, was a corporate lawyer; Henry Cabot Lodge comes from one of the oldest and most aristocratic of American families; Robert McNamara was president of the Ford Motor Company; Dean Rusk was president of the Rockefeller Foundation; Averell Harriman came from one of the richest railroad families in America; C. Douglas Dillon was head of one of Wall Street's big investment companies; McGeorge Bundy went from Harvard to the White House to the presidency of the Ford Foundation; Dean Acheson and Clark Clifford both were lawyers for the

richest corporate enterprises in America; Walt and Eugene
Rostow were sheltered academics at Yale—like many of
their colleagues, they are the "action intellectuals" so ad-
mired by Theodore White and much of the Washington press
corps before Vietnam.

In this sense, then, the core of our political premise—
the inequitable concentration of power—has implications for
American foreign policy. No less an authority than Lyndon
Johnson told us that "our foreign policy must always be an
extension of [the] nation's domestic policy"; that if you want
to know what we are doing abroad, look at what we are
doing at home. That is true, and we intend here to look at
four aspects of this policy: who decides foreign policy; who
bears the burden of that policy; how that policy must be
changed; and the ideological blindness that has afflicted both
the Right and the Left in America when they have looked
abroad.

We assert, first, that American foreign policy is the province of the privileged. This is not true for conspiratorial
reasons; it has far more to do with the urgent domestic
political goals of the dispossessed and the complexity of
world politics than with any cabal of Wall Street or Harvard.
But it has inevitable consequences. It means a confusion between the interest of American corporate power and the
"national interest" (on which our policy is always justified).
More fundamentally, it means a dangerous, numbing confi-
dence in American power by the men who exercise it. These
men are not losers. They have used wealth, or brains, or the
manipulation of the legal and political system to protect and
enhance their power. There is little understanding of frustration or complexity, or of the possibility that another force
may be strong enough to withstand their desires. And there
is little personal, experiential knowledge of what their decisions may mean to the people who must carry them out.

Thus Robert McNamara could assume that a rigid systems-
analysis approach would supply the scientifically correct de-

cisions for military pacification and social reform in Vietnam; it was a managerial problem, fundamentally similar to designing and pricing Ford automobiles. Apparently beyond the experience of a McNamara was the possibility that the National Liberation Front would not passively accept these decisions; the possibility that Saigon officials would feed Washington whatever statistics they thought would please their American underwriters.

Thus the Rostows and Bundys, out of lives spent with abstractions and words, could assume that an American-style constitution would fit the politics of South Vietnam. They could declare—with perfect doublethink—that it was necessary to combat the terror of guerrilla war with free-fire zones, massive population relocations, and American-trained assassination squads, and that this massive spilling of blood would aid in the creation of a world order, of a progressive community of nations. (Even in the late summer of 1971, as President Thieu was throwing opponents on and off the ballot like a puppeteer, Walt Rostow could write in *Look* magazine that the Saigon elections were proof of the worth of the American commitment.)

What we find especially objectionable is the mode of technocratic thinking and operating.

First, it is based on the arrogance of secrecy. In 1965 and 1966, the Bundys and Katzenbachs and Goldbergs told those of us who were marching against the Vietnam War that if only we knew what those wise men in government knew— if only we could read those secret cables and classified memos —we would not be in the streets. But when the Pentagon papers were leaked, it became clear that if we mortals had known the contents of those top-secret meetings and privileged documents—if we had known that the United States was poisoning the water supply of Hanoi in 1954 and encouraging commando raids into North Vietnam in 1956— we would have been in the streets a decade earlier.

Second, this type of thinking claims to be "value-free"

and "nonideological," but is not. Under the guise of intellectual neutrality, the foreign policy technocrats have concealed the most fundamental of biases: worldwide anticommunism, protection of capitalism, and a commitment to existing institutions. Just as the most rigid Marxists, they have used "historical inevitability" to disguise their ideology.*

Reading the memos and documents of the Pentagon papers, we are struck by the euphemisms invented to disguise, to sanitize, the deeds that were being advocated: "Protective reaction." "Sustained reprisal."

"Ordinance." "Surgical strike." "Fast full squeeze." Nowhere do we find "blood," "maimed," "homeless."

There is talk about "scenarios" and "options" and "relevant audiences."

The language is antiseptic. The words are abstract. Page after page of jargon dull the mind to the reality behind the words. So the authors never think of napalm searing flesh, of a GI with his genitals shot up, of a baby dead in a ditch. The whole bureaucratic system gives policy-makers the verbal camouflage and emotional detachment that enable them to be blind to the consequences of their acts.

Vietnam is of course the end of the road—the most visible, repellent consequence of the concepts supported and refined by the elitists who control our foreign policy. Yet there are other, less obvious but equally indefensible, examples of narrow reasoning. The American faith—only now coming under attack—is in bigness, union, conglomeration. And

---

* We must emphasize, however, that it is not our desire to make a blanket indictment of all intellectuals; nor do we wish to see, in any sense, a new era of anti-intellectualism. The first men to see the folly of Vietnam were also intellectuals—men like I. F. Stone, Howard Zinn, Marcus Raskin, and Senators Morse and Gruening. Our point here is limited to a special kind of intellectual who gravitates toward power, has a rigid set of cold war assumptions, comes out of a narrow network of elite institutions, and believes that only an elite group has the qualifications to make foreign policy. It is this special type who has controlled foreign policy for a generation and who, we believe, must be denied the privilege of governing again.

thus our foreign policy is a constant insistence on regional union: an Atlantic Union for Europe and America; CENTO and SEATO pacts for the Middle East and Southeast Asia; federation for Africa; and a Marshall Plan for every region of the underdeveloped world.

But does this notion make any sense abroad? Are the nations of Europe really one? Is regional union necessary for military security? Are the Latin American nations the same simply because their predominant language is Spanish? The question is always what is *real?* Abstractions, analogies, and illusions are no help. But the fact is that our foreign policy is overwhelmed by such dangerous baggage. Ho Chi Minh is Hitler; Ngo Dinh Diem (or is it Syngman Rhee or Chiang Kai-shek?) is Churchill—or maybe Roosevelt. The Marshall Plan can work in agrarian Asian societies, or feudal Latin American countries, because it worked in a Europe with two centuries of industrialization behind it. And always, always there is communism—the single, enormously powerful, essentially monolithic enemy to be opposed by whatever strength we can muster.

So ingrained is this response to a dangerous, confusing world—so rooted in the postwar European experience and so convenient a handle—that it has been used in situations that now seem ludicrous. In 1963, when a left-wing government came to power on the tiny African island of Zanzibar, we were solemnly warned that Castro and Cuba were going to intervene. The Stanleyville uprisings in the Congo in the early 1960's—product of cultural and tribal disputes completely obscure to America—were communist. A hundred political movements in the Third World, using the rhetoric of Marxism, have been seen as part of a communist international thrust. It is of a piece with Dean Rusk's contention in 1950 that the Chinese communist movement was a puppet state of the Kremlin: a "Slavic Manchukuo."

This is, of course, an oversimplified description. But no discussion of American foreign policy can stray from the central fact that the men who make it come from the top; they talk and meet with each other; they draw on a set of experiences so common as to be homogeneous; and they find security in the assumptions and convictions each shares. The consequence is more than social: for the other America has paid dearly for this closed society of foreign policy-makers.

In November of 1966, Pat Moynihan argued in the *New Republic* that the army was an ideal tool for enlistment in the War on Poverty. At about the same time, Defense Department figures revealed that black casualties in Vietnam were running *double* the ratio of blacks in America. In a perverse sense, Moynihan was right: for in Vietnam, an authentic coalition of blacks and working-class whites was taking shape; a coalition that exists today in military cemeteries and the paraplegic wards of Veterans Administration hospitals. Within a year, the fathers and brothers of these victims were to be hit with a 10 per cent surcharge on their income tax to help pay for the war in Vietnam—a tax whose flat rate was effectively an exemption for the upper 10 per cent of American taxpayers.

This is nothing new. In the summer of 1950, shortly after the outbreak of the Korean War, John Foster Dulles summoned America to sacrifice in the pages of the *New York Times Magazine:*

> The time for sacrifice and discipline is here. . . . Most of us will have to work longer hours and with more intensity. We shall all have to give up some material enjoyments and be more frugal in our living. There will be fewer automobiles, television sets and gadgets to buy and there will be bigger tax bills to pay.

The same sort of words could be used to describe the nobility working Americans are urged to adopt in bearing the costs of a foreign policy with which they have had nothing to do. There was no excess profits tax during the Vietnam

War; there was no universal military service. Instead, the lower end of the economic spectrum went off to war and saw its real income cut (between 1965 and 1970, real weekly take-home pay of the American worker dropped by 96 cents). Draft deferments went to college and graduate students, and to those whose education enabled them to get draft-exempt jobs. There were no 2-A and 2-S deferments for the gas station attendant, or the steelworker. They, and the poor of Appalachia, and the blacks and Puerto Ricans and Chicanos from the hidden corners of America were mobilized to fight the war that had been conceived in Harvard Yard.

It is tragically true that the institutions that claimed to speak for the working American have consistently failed to resist the foreign policy of the elite. The AFL-CIO has been a consistent supporter of American foreign policy; under George Meany and his foreign policy aide Jay Lovestone, it has embraced every element of hysterical anticommunism; it has used CIA funds to help foment labor strikes and thus unseat Cheddi Jagan in Guyana; it has at times tried to make its own foreign policy, by permitting New York longshoremen's unions to boycott ships trading with communist nations.

It is true, also, that intellectuals who insisted on political coalitions with the union movement compromised themselves by embracing the cold war foreign policy. At the height of the Vietnam War, Bayard Rustin and Pat Moynihan were urging liberals to support Lyndon Johnson instead of fighting him politically on the war issue.

But this blindness cannot disguise the fact the poor pay for American foreign policy. War means inflation—and the powerless pay for that. War means, ultimately, economic dislocation. And, as we are still learning, the poor pay most for that. And beyond these economic costs, it is the powerless who spill their guts out on foreign beaches and jungles to fulfill the assertions of the Bundys and Rostows and Kissingers and Dulleses; it is the poor who live out their lives without arms and legs and faces. If there is any purpose at all to war crimes investigations, if there is any "sentence" to be placed on the men who led us to war, it would be to spend an hour a day in St. Albans or Walter Reed—meeting the maimed face to face, and telling them of the worldwide Great Society they hoped to build. It may be that this kind of research could force those who hold power to make the connection between their policies and the real costs of those policies for America.

And it may be that this kind of investigation—this kind of personal involvement—would enable America to begin evaluating realistically its military-defense empire. The idea that a single airplane can cost $2 billion more than it should, or that $25 billion in weaponry was utterly wasted over the last fifteen years is a sick joke. And to the out-of-work engineer who is told there are no jobs for him, to the 35-cent-an-hour farm worker who is told there are no schools and homes for him, to the men and women on the scrap heap of America's neglected work, this kind of foreign policy consequence must stand as the ultimate repudiation.

In this sense, then, the loss of power by the foreign policy elite may well be another kind of redistribution of wealth; it may transfer public funds from building the illusions of the elite into building the homes and the hopes of the dispossessed.

No one can set down inflexible rules for foreign policy; that attempt has been the bane of American policy. We can, however, suggest ground rules for a foreign policy more in the interest of the majority of Americans:

ONE   **An unfriendly or ideologically hostile government is not necessarily a threat to the United States**

For ten years, elements of America's leadership have paid lip service to this idea, and we no longer insist the world is menaced by a single, monolithic communist movement. Yet our real policy has been otherwise. Every postwar president has used American imperial power to consolidate the overthrow of unfriendly governments—none of them in any sense a Soviet satellite. The examples range from Mossadegh in Iran to Arbenz in Guatemala, from Cheddi Jagan in Guyana to Diem in South Vietnam and Sihanouk in Cambodia.

We do not recommend this policy change for ideological reasons. Such a change is vital because our identification with client states is a source of constant danger to us—danger of gradual involvement with the survival of a particular government, or opposition to a particular leader, which threatens to drag us into war.

TWO **We must stop seeing foreign nations through the eyes of our own political judgments**

If the Duvalier family declared Haiti a "people's republic" tomorrow and replaced pictures of Papa Doc with posters of Che, Marx, and Lenin, two things would happen immediately: first, a committee of artists, writers, and intellectuals would form a "Hands Off Haiti" committee and write pieces in the *New York Review of Books* explaining that the *tonton macoutes* are really a people's militia; second, seventy-five Republican Congressmen would demand "immediate, effective action to rid us of this menace 125 miles from our shores."

We do not make real judgments about foreign policy. Instead, we root for one country or another, like so many football fans. This is a failing of Right and Left alike. Moise Tshombe defends private enterprise and calls himself an anticommunist; the Young Americans for Freedom hold a rally for him. The Syrian dictatorship calls itself socialist—and American radicals embrace this tin-horn police state.

This kind of response to rhetoric is juvenile. It is also dangerous, because it is the enemy of clear thought. A country is not a democracy because it calls itself one; it is not socialist because it assails imperialism; it is not a friend of America because it throws *our* enemies in jail.

An example: Many Americans want this country to withdraw recognition of the Greek regime because of its oppressive policies. Many of these same Americans have supported trade, diplomatic recognition, and U.N. membership for mainland China: an oppressive, dictatorial regime. (There are, of course, other Americans who want to continue to isolate China and to maintain friendship with Greece.) As far as their commitments to democracy are concerned, the distinctions between these dictatorships are meaningless. They are both unpleasant regimes—Greece is no better because it is anticommunist, and China is no better because its dictatorship is egalitarian.

A sensible foreign policy—one that would best serve the majority of Americans—would face the facts of both regimes; would extend diplomatic recognition to both, and military aid to neither. Such a policy would be honest enough to acknowledge the effective control of both regimes and the oppressive aspects of both. It would start a war with neither government —and go to war on behalf of neither government.

THREE   Take the profit out of national defense

Every time a new weapons systems is debated, a legion of former armed forces brass, now employed as lobbyists for electronics, aerospace, and other defense-related industries, swarms all over Washington to argue that the national defense requires a nuclear-powered airplane, or an ABM, or an Advanced Manned Strategic Aircraft, or an atomic K-Ration, or whatever is now on the drawing boards. We are told these weapons are essential. Fine. But if they are, let the companies build them at cost; with no profit to themselves.

FOUR   Make the draft equitable

We do not countenance a draft that exempts the children of the privileged and drags in the children of the powerless. We would end totally all student deferments, including those affecting the children of U.S. congressmen; and we would keep the draft at minimal levels in peacetime. The business, academic, and political community should constantly be aware that if our leadership drags us into war, their children will be as vulnerable as those of the dispossessed.

FIVE   Stop equating corporate interest with national interest

The interests of American corporations in the markets and resources of underdeveloped nations have had a deep effect on foreign policy. Oil in Iran, sugar in Cuba, United Fruit in Guatemala are recent examples of investments dominating policy. We can afford no more.

SIX   Immediate and total withdrawal from Indochina

The war in Indochina is not over. It is true that fewer Americans are in Vietnam—but the bombing, the maiming, and the murder have been accelerated and expanded into three nations.

We must demand all candidates support withdrawal—and by that we mean no residual force in Vietnam, no CIA operation in Laos, no bombing of the North, no aid to mercenaries in Thailand, no support for Thieu. And no political strategy of appealing to working-class "patriotic" sentiment can override the moral imperative of opposing the Indochina war.

14 ★ Opening Up the Political Process

In March, 1971, with inflation at a ten-year high, and with food budgets putting millions of American families in a desperate financial squeeze, the Nixon administration was faced with a decision directly affecting food prices. Big dairy interests were urging the Department of Agriculture to boost the price of "manufactured milk"—a commodity vital to making many dairy products. A price hike, according to a former economic adviser of Nixon's, would "increase food prices by hundreds of millions of dollars."

Secretary of Agriculture Hardin refused to allow the price increase; he could find no reason to justify an increase that would so directly threaten the economic welfare of so many people.

A few days after the Hardin decision, about a dozen major dairy representatives met behind closed doors with President Nixon. There was no public announcement that a major economic decision was in the making; no open debate; nobody was there from labor or the poor; there were no consumer representatives or economists. And there is no written record to study, or correct, or challenge in court or Congress or federal agency.

Instead, two days after the meeting, the dairy industry got its price increase; the Secretary of Agriculture said "new evidence" had shown the need for the price hike. Almost immediately, the kind of new evidence that President Nixon took to heart became clear. A series of political committees were established in the District of Columbia—where reporting and disclosure laws have more loopholes than Swiss cheese—with names like Americans for Greater Public Awareness, the League of Involved Citizens, and the Committee for Political Integrity. The names sounded different, but in two vital ways the groups were identical: first, they had no existence, no function except to collect large chunks of cash from those dairymen who benefited financially from the higher prices for manufactured milk. (Since the law *does* limit the amount of campaign gifts, each committee collected its "limit.") Second, all of the cash collected by these dummy organizations went into the same pocket: a Washington organization called the Committee for the Re-Nomination of the President.

Why the Committee for the Re-*Nomination* of the President instead of "re-election"? Because under federal law, primary campaigns are exempt from most campaign spending limits and from disclosure regulations. But if the funds aren't needed for primary fights, they can be carried over into the general election—something the Nixon administration could logically assume would happen, given the likelihood of Nixon's renomination.

The contributions from these dairy interests had already topped $250,000 by the time the *Wall Street Journal* broke the story in the fall of 1971. By election time, the *Journal* said, more than $1 million would find its way from the dairy interests into the Nixon re-election treasury.

The train of events tells a lot about the corruption of the political process. Government decisions are basic to the distribution of wealth and power, especially given the enormous control government exercises over the economic life of America: Congress, the president, and the federal and state agencies decide who pays how much in taxes, whose products are protected from foreign and new domestic competitors, how intensively the antitrust laws will be used, who will get defense contracts worth billions of dollars, what foreign nations will be threatened with reprisals for nationalizing American-owned businesses, what rate of return is fair for telephone and electric companies, and whether deceptive advertising will be punished or ignored.

As it stands now, the political process forms a kind of closed circle with economic power. Because wealth—or access to wealth—is critical to gaining political power, those who make the basic decisions are often beholden to the people and institutions who already hold economic power. The citizens who are the victims of economic power are often shut out of the process by which real decisions are made; for while the public can organize and use its voting power, the most critical decisions are made in congressional committees and federal agencies, which are essentially unreachable except by groups with economic leverage.

We disagree completely with the accusation that the American political process is a fraud. Too many fights have been won in the past—from collective bargaining for labor to civil rights legislation to the repudiation of the Vietnam War—to believe that the system of representative democracy is unworkable. But what is true is that *we must lessen the impact of economic power on political decisions.* As long as the key congressmen and executive decision-makers are spokesmen for entrenched wealth, fairness is an impossibility. The fix is in as much as if a judge had a direct economic interest in a case he was deciding.

It was ten years ago that the Port Huron Statement, the founding document of SDS, made an eloquent plea for "participatory democracy." Yet America has not achieved representative democracy. The immediate goal must be to democratize the democratic process.

The connection between wealth and politics isn't as blatant as it was in the late nineteenth and early twentieth centuries, when, as David Graham Philipps charged in his muckraking classic *The Treason of the Senate,* large corporations simply paid huge cash sums to congressmen for their votes on critical issues like tariffs or rights of way. But the link is still direct enough—and dangerous enough—to make reform of the political process an important issue on the agenda of the new populism.

The first area of reform must be the electoral process itself. As it stands now, it costs so much money to run candidates for office that either personal wealth or access to great wealth are the most important qualifications for office.

In 1968, Richard Nixon spent more than $25 million to win the presidency; in 1972, he will probably spend $50 million, not even counting the millions of dollars in free publicity his office assures him, the free time he can commandeer on all TV and radio networks for addresses to the nation, and a president's capacity to manipulate federal spending— dams, missile contracts, Model City grants—to win votes.

This incredible level of spending pervades politics from the White House to Congress and on to state legislatures. The enormous cost and importance of television is one critical factor; according to the Federal Communications Commission, in the 1968 elections, the cost for all political commercials—which includes the costs for air time and for producing commercials—was $90 million. A single network one-minute commercial on a highly rated show can near $100,000. (The total costs of all electioneering in 1968 hit an unbelievable total of $300 million—a 50 per cent increase over 1964.)

These costs have made campaigning for any office the province of the weathy. Nelson Rockefeller's 1970 campaign to retain the governor's office cost between $10 and $20 million. In fact, in that New York election, three of the six candidates for statewide office were millionaires—Rockefeller, James Buckley, and his unsuccessful Democratic opponent for the Senate, Congressman Richard Ottinger.

In the only congressional election in 1971, for a seat in the Pittsburgh suburbs, both office-seekers were millionaires. In 1968, a candidate for the New York State Assembly— Andrew Stein, the son of a millionaire—*reported* spending more than $250,000 for that local office. It cost John Tunney and George Murphy more than $2 million each to campaign for the Senate seat from California, and in North Dakota, well outside expensive "media markets," the Republican candidate for the Senate spent—officially— $300,000 in his losing effort. In 1968, according to Herbert Alexander's study *Financing the 1968 Election,* twelve of America's richest families gave $2.76 million to political aspirants—all but $150,000 of which went to Republicans. (The Rockefellers alone gave $1.7 million to Governor Rockefeller's unsuccessful campaign for the Republican presidential nomination.) And these are only the official, reported figures.

Campaign inflation is a national scandal. It has, according to one study, pushed the cost per vote in a national election from 19 cents in 1952 to 60 cents in 1968. And what this means, increasingly, is that without money, a candidate cannot run for office. Whether his politics are conservative or liberal, he must appeal to *some* monied sources—or be shut out.

The impact of wealth on politics was highlighted in November of 1971, when a series of $500-a-plate dinners brought in *$5 million* to the war chest of President Nixon in a *single night.* The oil industry alone bought about $200,000 worth of tickets to help re-elect the man who preserved the outrageous $5 billion oil import quota scheme. Under the election laws, almost none of this money need be reported; and names of the big contributors will never be known to the public.

Sometimes the connection between economic interests and political campaigns is clearcut; as in 1968, when Hubert Humphrey refused to commit himself to protecting the oil depletion allowance and Richard Nixon pledged to maintain it. The oilmen cut Humphrey off and swelled Nixon's campaign treasury. Sometimes, to avoid running afoul of the Corrupt Practices Act, it is done through special committees like the American Medical Political Action Committee (AMPAC), which channeled money to candidates and incumbents opposing government-sponsored health care; or the Bankers Political Action Committee (BPAC), which in 1970, kicked in $200,000 to members of the Senate Finance and House Ways and Means Committees who were friendly to bankers. Organized labor has its own tool for avoiding the law, the Committee on Political Education (COPE). And unions have used their economic strength to influence politics, sometimes by violating the rights of their members. The Marine Engineers Beneficial Association takes $10 a month from the pensions of its retirees—and at times from the widows of dead members—which goes to help politicians friendly to maritime unions. The 1,750 pensioners "voluntarily" kicked in $224,000 to give to 120 candidates for Congress. (In a spirit of generosity, $60,000-a-year union officials gave as much as $3,780-a-year pensioneers.) In a technique used by both business and labor alike, organizations offer exorbitant fees for the speeches of legislators. Maryland's Charles Mathias earned $2,000 for a speech of 905 words to the Marine Engineers Training School. But the fund-raising capacities of labor cannot match those of business and financial interests. Its primary way of helping is to use workers for canvassing and local organizing.

But so prevalent, and so critical, is the role of money in political campaigns that Congress and the executive often functions as they did when the muckrakers spoke of "the Senator from Standard Oil" or "the gentlemen from the Sugar Trust." And thus the first critical step in opening the political process is to reduce the role of money in political campaigns.

This cannot be done only by putting a ceiling on spending for radio and television. Important as it is to control who gets on the air and how, it is not enough. That kind of limit only means more money will be spent on less visible, but equally dangerous, political devices—like the direct-mail computer letter to selected ethnic and economic interest groups, or straight cash payments to voters and political leaders.

Instead, we suggest reform along these lines:

ONE   **An absolute limit on total campaign spending, with mandatory criminal penalties for violation, as well as the nullification of any election in which the victorious candidate violated the spending ceiling**

These ceilings, calculated at so many cents per vote, would cover total campaign spending, from office staffs to posters to print advertising to telephone and door-to-door canvassers. The provision that an election would be canceled if the winner broke the law might at least encourage an end to the gentlemen's agreement now prevailing, in which neither party goes after the other's dishonest devices for fear that their own would be discovered.

TWO   **A complete ban on all radio and TV advertising, with stations required to give free equal time to all candidates**

The devices of "media manipulators" and "image packagers" may well be questionable techniques, but it is doubtful they are any more dishonest than the universal use of ghostwritten speeches and position papers that a candidate can't even understand much less write himself. What is dangerous and completely intolerable is the cost of buying time that puts so much weight on the side of money.

A rule forbidding the purchase of time and requiring the provision of free equal time would let candidates deliver their messages as they choose—in one-minute spots, five-minute speeches, or half-hour shows in which listeners phoned in their questions. It would not end the use of image techniques, but the unfair advantages of wealth, which let a man like Nelson Rockefeller outspend his opponents 20-1, would no longer be in effect.

THREE   **Make contributors as well as candidates criminally liable for breaking the law on contributions**

A corporate executive who lends a company plane to a candidate or who loans out a subordinate to work on a campaign while being paid by the company is a contributor. So is a union that absorbs the printing costs of a political brochure. So is a rich family that foots the bill for hotel rooms or dinners. All of these contributions should be counted in any calculation of campaign spending. And both politicians and contributors should be punished for breaking the law if they do not report and disclose these kinds of hidden subsidies.

Such reforms are themselves subject to evasion. If, for example, a separate ceiling were set up for primaries, a candidate like Rockefeller might well finance a phony primary opponent to enable him to put more of his own commercials on the air. And effective enforcement would require substantial political courage at the state or federal levels. But a start must be made to keep "one man, one vote" from becoming "one dollar, one vote."

Election spending is the most dramatic example of needed reforms. There are others, which we will touch on briefly.

FOUR   **Require that legislators disclose all of their financial interests that would be affected by legislation on which they speak and vote**

The late Senator Everett Dirksen, beloved by television newsmen for his colorful speech, was one of the most venal men ever to sit in the Senate. While he spoke out for every special interest conceivable, his Peoria, Illinois law firm paid him money for referring such clients as pipeline and paper companies to the firm. It was Dirksen who used piously to object to rules that would force senators to reveal where their money came from, arguing that such rules would make them "second class citizens."

While Dirksen was more blatant than most congressmen, direct conflicts of interest pervade the House and Senate. Russell Long, whose otherwise firm stand against special interests turns to Jello in the face of the gas and oil lobby, is the principal spokesman for the special tax privileges and other financial bonanzas of oil and gas companies. He is also better off by hundreds of thousands of dollars thanks to his oil interests. James Eastland, who is a key senator in determining agricultural policies, has made almost $150,000 per year thanks to the farm subsidy program. Oklahoma's late Senator Robert Kerr was the wealthiest man in Congress because of the oil holdings he protected as Senate Finance Chairman. Jacob Javits, a respected "liberal" whose law firm represented many big banks and financial interests, was Wall Street's principal advocate in the Senate.*

In fact, an outright majority of congressmen have such conflicts. More than 300 of them have financial interests in law firms that represent banks, real estate companies, gas and oil firms, and insurance companies. Many of these law firms, although located in small towns, are retained by corporate giants with huge legal staffs—not so coincidentally because the congressmen who earn income from these firms wield power in Washington. More than 90 congressmen have direct fi-

---

* Shortly after his brother was suspended from legal practice because of unethical behavior, Javits announced he was severing ties with his firm because of desires to avoid a "conflict of interest"—presumably, fifteen years in the Senate had not created such conflicts.

nancial interests in banks; bank profits are determined directly by national fiscal and economic policies.

Ideally, we believe no one should sit in Congress with such clear possible conflicts of interest. A $40,000-a-year income plus the many perquisities of congressional office ought to be enough for a moderate level of income. Many congressmen and senators, such as William Proxmire, former Senators Paul Douglas and Albert Gore, and others serve their people well without any such ties.

But given the fact that a congressman can be as venal as the next man (if not more so), the least that can be done is to require congressmen—and, by extension, state legislators as well—to reveal exactly what their finances are in relation to crucial votes.

It would be refreshing to hear a congressman "declare his interest" and state:

"Mr. Speaker, this bill is un-American, bolshevistic, bureaucratic, and the enemy of progress. I also calculate it would cost me $15,000 in dividends from private utility stock."

FIVE   Open up and decentralize decision-making in federal agencies

We have discussed elsewhere our recommendations about regulatory agencies. But it is important to remember that the decisions of these agencies are *political;* they decide who gets benefits and who doesn't. And frequently, the whole process is closed off to the public. Decisions are made in Washington, hundreds or thousands of miles from communities affected by such items as TV-license renewals, airline franchises, and power plants. These political matters are so closed, and often so expensive—a single administrative hearing can cost anywhere from $5,000 to $100,000 in legal fees and costs—that people and organizations without money are often totally ignored.

We believe that any agency decision affecting local communities should be taken only after an affirmative effort has been made to sample sentiment in those communities. If the Federal Power Commission is going to authorize a power plant that will hurt the ecology of a region, it should hold hearings in that region; it should reveal its intentions, instead of hiding them in fine print in the *Federal Register*. TV and radio licenses should be renewed only after local hearings.

SIX   **Communities, neighborhoods, and towns must be given greater say in the decisions about their own futures and in the operation of government services**

These matters are, in the broadest sense, political: how schools are run, how a neighborhood is to be renewed, how police, courts, and hospitals function. But too often, ordinary people feel alienated, powerless to affect government conduct. Houses are bulldozed, expressways built; sanitation collections are reduced, new street lights don't get installed, a new hospital doesn't get approved. These are the sorts of decisions local communities should have a role in making and implementing.

Recently, we became involved in a fight in Corona, Queens, to stop the tearing down of sixty-nine homes in order to build a high school athletic field. The homeowners were all Italian-Americans with little political clout. The City Planning Commission ignored the neighborhood's desires. The builder, realty interests, and the Board of Education bureaucracy were in favor of the athletic field. The sixty-nine homeowners had no say in the matter. Only when demonstrations were organized and the *Village Voice* and the *New York Post* began to write about the story, did the city administration change its mind and save the homes.

It is our contention that community boards—elected by local neighborhoods and served by professional staffs—should have the dominant role in setting priorities and making local planning decisions. We also think elected community boards should have the major voice in the running of some local institutions—schools and hospitals. (Although not courts or police. If law has any meaning, it must be consistent; homosexuality cannot be a capital offense in a working-class neighborhood and compulsory in a counterculture neighborhood.) We believe this process would provide more rational and democratic decision-making. And it would improve municipal services, because accountability would be clear and buckpassing through the bureaucratic maze would be more difficult.

But we must emphasize that decentralization is not the universal panacea some of its proponents make it out to be. It does not alter wealth or re-allocate funds. If there is no money to build and staff a new hospital, then a community board with power to set policy on abortions and methadone programs is meaningless. Without the economic resources and budget-making power, community participation becomes an empty slogan, a faddish *cul de sac*.

Enthusiasts of the purer forms of community *control* must also face up to the irony that local control in places like Alabama, or Cicero, Illinois, could mean racism by democratic choice; for this reason, some *national* policies must prevail on moral grounds.

SEVEN   **Party reform—democratizing the process of nominating a candidate for president—is imperative**

In 1968, Hubert Humphrey did not win a single presidential primary—but he was nominated by the Democratic convention. In the primaries, 8 million Democrats showed their opposition to the Vietnam War by voting for either Robert Kennedy or Eugene McCarthy. But the convention delegates, controlled by unions and picked by local leaders, voted down an antiwar platform plank. This happened because the 8 million who voted in the primaries had less actual power at the convention than a dozen political and labor leaders.

The McGovern (now Fraser) Commission has drawn up guidelines to unrig the nominating process. The proposals are sound and sensible: no delegate can be chosen before the calendar year of the convention. Each delegation must have a fair proportion of women, blacks, young people, and other minorities. The political parties must adopt and publish written rules for the delegate selection process. The unit rule must be abolished. All delegates must be elected, either in a primary or a state convention.

Most big industrial states have not yet complied with these reforms. And it now seems likely that Lawrence O'Brien, George Meany, Richard Daley, and a few governors will be able to control the 1972 Democratic convention, despite the large number of primaries. As in 1968, the ordinary people who vote in the primaries may end up powerless to affect the outcome.

A bad process produces good candidates only by accident. If any political party in the country is to earn allegiances, it will have to make the McGovern recommendations permanent policy—in practice, not just on paper.

EIGHT **Automatic voter registration of everyone at eighteen**

The poor and the powerless still encounter barriers to voting. Automatic enrollment would cut through the red tape and increase participation. One side effect: more blacks on juries, which are picked from voter lists.

These are the kinds of reforms we think can make a difference. There are others, such as lessening the impact of the seniority system in Congress, although it is by no means clear that a total end to seniority will bring better congressional behavior: seniority has given us Mendel Rivers and James Eastland, but it has also put people like Estes Kefauver, Phil Hart, Gaylord Nelson, and Edward Kennedy in positions of responsibility. Meanwhile, the alernative—straight party caucuses—gave us Robert Byrd, one of the most mean-spirited men in modern Senate history, as Majority Whip. What is true is that committee chairmen must not continue to have the arbitrary and capricious power to push through or block legislation on their own whims.

The thrust of our argument, however, is that this political system can be made to operate more fairly. In order to judge basic questions of wealth and power, we must break the vicious circle by which economic power controls so much political power, which in turn protects economic power.

Part Three ★ A New Majority for Justice

15 ★ The Making of a New Majority

THIS BOOK is essentially an argument; a case for a single proposition (wealth and power are illegitimately distributed in America) supported by specific evidence about our economic and political life. It comes out of a belief that a political coalition which makes the fight for fairness its goal can be built in America in the immediate political future.

It is critical, however, to separate what we *want* to happen from what we *think* will happen politically. Without question, a populist coalition is only one possibility of many; and if we have learned anything from 1968, it is that no one can predict the future course of politics.

The willingness to make the wish father to the thought seems to grip most discussions of coming political change, including three books that have received considerable attention: *The Greening of America,* by Charles A. Reich; *The Emerging Republican Majority,* by Kevin Phillips; and *The Real Majority,* by Richard Scammon and Benjamin Wattenberg. Each sees history moving inevitably its own way.

Each of these books, we believe, is substantially flawed as

a work of political analysis. We will try to show why, and, in so doing, present the case for a new populist coalition as a political reality.

The Greening of America is a lot of books in one; a book about economic and political history, a book about cultural radicalism, a book about peanut butter. It reads at times as if it had been written by a very bright college freshman from a small town in Kentucky dazzled by his first look at an Ivy League campus, the night before it was due as a term paper and while its author was heavily under the influence of the *cannabis* leaf. There are brilliant insights, dozens of internal contradictions, eager bursts of hopefulness, callow—sometimes stupid—generalizations, thoughtful discussions of social institutions, and inane discussions of politics.

While most reviewers assailed the book, it seemed to touch a nerve with affluent white liberals seeking to hear what it was that "the kids are trying to tell us." Both *Rolling Stone* and *Fortune* magazine welcomed it; and the constituencies of both had good reason for doing so.

For the central *political* message of *Greening* is: "Cool it. You don't have to do anything except what you're already doing and the corporate state is dead." Reich states—explicitly —that a change in lifestyle (or "consciousness") will by itself change the politics of America. There will be no battles, no efforts to retain wealth and power, no sacrifices—for sacrifice is an archaic remnant of Consciousness II. Instead, one day we will wake to find that Con III is in control of the FBI, General Motors, Harvard University, AT&T, the Plumbers' Union, the Ford Foundation, and the Cosa Nostra.

Reich calls *Greening* a "work of fiction." It is, in fact, a fairy tale—literally—in the way it approaches politics. Reich himself says, "when self is recovered"—that is, when Con III is within enough of us—"the corporate state will be ended, as miraculously as a kiss breaks a witch's evil enchantment."

It is hard to write about the political texture of *Greening* without creating the suspicion that we are distorting the book's ideas. But Reich *does* believe that all of the traditional approaches to politics are not only failures but irrelevant; that labor leaders, student activists, the Kennedys, and presumably squares like Martin Luther King and I. F. Stone, are hopelessly trapped in the old-fashioned, Puritan, self-defeating world of Consciousness II. And he *does* believe that the questions of wealth and power are not the basic political questions at all. He says:

> There is no class struggle; today, there is only one class. . . . We are all the proletariat, and there is no longer any ruling class except the machine itself . . . there is nobody whatever on the other side. Nobody wants inadequate housing and medical care, only the machine. Nobody wants war, except the machine. And even businessmen, once liberated, would like to roll in the grass and lie in the sun. There is no need to fight against any group of people in America. . . .
>
> All that is necessary to describe the new society is to describe a new way of life. . . . This is not avoiding the hard questions. The hard questions—if by that is meant political and economic organization—are insignificant, even irrelevant.

In the words of Con III's "ultimate sign of reverence, vulnerability, and innocence," oh wow!

Since Reich believes that the new revolution will originate "with the individual and with culture, and . . . will change the political structure only as its final act," it is important to recognize how inaccurately Reich has read the youth culture that is to bring on this revolution. In describing the wonders of Con III, the passionate prose with which Reich indicts the corporate state turns into the simperings of an Adela Rogers St. John. Con III, as far as can be sorted out, seems to be an amalgam of rock music, drugs, love beads, hitchhikers, long hair, communes, drab colors (they reflect nature), bright colors (they reflect sensuality), polymorphous sex, Peace Corps volunteers (presumably exempted from the "sacrificer" tag that taints Con II reformists), Ken Kesey, real peanut butter, and bell-bottoms, provided they are bought cheap. The Con III community—which according to Reich sprang up in the late '60's among the young and is now spreading throughout the land—is a fantasy as unreal as the college musical of the 1930's in which coeds and campus heroes strolled along the green, humming in perfect harmony. It is the Kids as a lonely middle-ager might choose to see them: loving, generous, honest, nonmaterialistic, loving, faithful, sensual, and loving.*

But those of us who have spent even a modest amount of time in the East Village, Taos, Berkeley, or Madison, Wisconsin have seen a darker shade of greening: fifteen-year-old runaways strung out on dope; syphilis and gonorrhea becoming epidemics; heroin and methadrine addicts turning the countercommunities into jungles; minds destroyed by LSD; rock music and its artifacts controlled by conglomerate corporations and hucksters in wide ties and love beads; Abbie Hoffman ripping off his friends and companions out of book royalties; underground newspapers proclaiming Charles Manson as "Man of the Year"; Jerry Rubin huckstering a violence trip he prudently will not take; Fillmore longhairs mockingly offering flowers to the East European immigrant elderly trying to keep Tompkins Square Park as a sanctuary for their neighborhood in New York's East Village; A. J. Weberman stealing Bob Dylan's garbage and ordering him to write ideologically correct songs, and then —inevitably—foraying into the garbage of celebrities for *Esquire* magazine; Hell's Angels outbrutalizing the Chicago

---

* In discussing the friendliness of the Kids, Reich says "it is as if, in the old college days, the whole football team had come knocking at the scrawny freshman's door, saying 'join us,' 'we're your friends,' 'come to our parties.' " (p. 268). This single sentence may explain far more than Reich intended it ·to.

police at Altamont; and Janis Joplin, Jimi Hendrix, Brian Jones all dead from drugs.

In the end, youth culture revealed its flaw, undetected in the 400 pages of *Greening:* that it is composed of human beings who are subject to the same weaknesses and temptations as every other group of human beings. The yogis, yippies, and youthfreaks turned out, if anything, to be portents of a decaying social order, not heralders of a new vanguard. And, despite Reich's insistence that the Con III tribe "just knows" great truths, its cultural contributions have been far less enduring than those of, say, Hannah Arendt, or Erik Erikson, or Norman Mailer, or Stanley Kubrick.

The short, unhappy life of the youth culture is critical to the validity of *Greening* because Reich insists that culture is politics. His vision, evidently, is that sooner or later the Secretary of Defense, the chairman of the board of U.S. Steel, and every other spokesman for power is going to pull off his $17.50 tie and $300 suit, don a tie-dyed shirt and bell-bottom jeans, and liberate his institution; it's a kind of universalization of Scrooge at the end of *A Christmas Carol.* But in political terms, this is literally meaningless. In Reich's own terms, it is the machine itself—the institution—that is the issue. If the chairman of the board becomes a convert, will he announce that the corporation's dividends are to be used to finance a day-care center program? Or that workers in his plant will have the chance for paid sabbaticals? Or that the capital gains section of the tax laws will no longer be used by his corporation's executives? And if so, how much longer will he hold his position of power?

The whole point of politics—a point raised by Reich and then ignored—is that no sane society trusts solely to the good will of its inhabitants. To say that "if we all were Con IIIs, we would need no laws" is a tautology—by Reich's definition, all Con IIIs are amorally pure and completely trustworthy. It is like saying, "If we were all pure Christians, all our political difficulties would cease"—and just about as likely to happen.

Indeed, in this sense, Reich is the Billy Graham of the affluent concerned liberals. Just as Graham tells chamber of commerce leaders that they are moral, serving Christ their own way, Reich tells the disaffected children of the well-off to "drop-out," "do your thing"—and the world will follow.

But what of the people who do not frequent the dining halls of Yale University? How do you tell a forty-eight-year-old sanitation worker that "any job [is] a potential opportunity for self-expression, for play"? If you mean that he should have the right to work at his own pace, or pursue other interests, then the question is: how does he win that kind of life? What kinds of programs and institutional changes will be needed to make that kind of life possible? For the jobless black, for the seventy-five-year-old woman living out her life in the waiting rooms of bus and train stations, searching for some sign of human affection, for the cop making $8,000 a year and the inmate of the Tombs denied the right to a shower, *The Greening of America* is like the thousands of Americans who sent tons of potato chips and snack foods to Biafrans starving to death; the gesture was well-meaning, but it wasn't the right kind of help to sustain life. A decade from now, if it is still the fashion, we will see fifty-year-old bankers, board chairmen, and slumlords dancing to rock music under psychedelic lights and pausing for an occasional toke on a righteous joint. And the air and rivers will still be poisoned; and children still will go hungry; and men will spend their lives working for far less than they deserve.

It is Kevin Phillips's contention that Richard Nixon will fundamentally reshape American politics the way Franklin Roosevelt did, by creating a new, enduring coalition—"the emerging Republican majority"—which will foreshadow "a new Republican era."

According to Phillips's shrewd and at times scary book, this new GOP majority will be built on a racist populism, and include six different constituencies: the Wallace voters (13 per cent in 1968), the South ("southern strategy"), the growing "sun belt" cities (San Diego, Phoenix, Albuquerque, Houston, Tulsa, and Orlando), working-class Catholics, "the heartlands," and "the ordinary suburbs."*

We agree there is conservative potential in all these groupings, and Phillips does have a deep understanding of what motivates certain people. But we think he overstates his case, and that he overlooks countervailing trends that will more than neutralize the magnets pulling voters to the Right.

First, Phillips takes the Wallace vote for granted as a monolithic part of his new GOP majority. The facts do not support this assumption. In the North, surveys have shown that many Wallace voters originally favored Robert Kennedy as their "anti-Establishment" candidate. And in the South, within the same party it is going to be hard to reconcile poor, rural farmers and the upper-class, anti-union suburban types who elected William Brock in Tennessee. In Alabama, Wallace himself likes to needle the "country club set" that is behind Nixon's former Postmaster, Winton Blount. Phillips seems occasionally aware of this contradiction, and his newspaper columns show a fear of a resurgent southern populism that would attract lower-class Wallace voters back to the Democrats. (The assumption Nixon could draw Wallace supporters also fails to take into account the irrational and cultural factors in voting behavior. Putting his politics aside, Wallace is an attractive campaigner, and undoubtedly many people voted for him just because he did appear plain-spoken, tough, and earthy; these are not qualities to be found in Richard Nixon.)

Phillips's southern strategy was punctured by the 1970

* Phillips says bluntly: "The GOP can build a winning coalition without Negro votes."

election results, which provided clear evidence that no inexorable, long-term trend toward the GOP exists in the South. In 1970, the Democrats elected new, moderate governors in Florida, Georgia, Arkansas, and South Carolina. The Democrats also increased their majority in the North Carolina state legislature, and in 1971 they regained the Kentucky governorship.

Phillips's assertion that urban Catholics are moving into the Republican Party is also yet to be proven. In 1970, Catholics voted for James Buckley and Tom Dodd as independent candidates. In Massachusetts, they voted for Ted Kennedy as a Democrat. In short, ethnicity and religion seem to be variables independent of party or ideology.

There are also important factors that Phillips inexplicably ignores in his analysis. One is the 11 million newly enfranchised voters between eighteen and twenty-one, and the 25 million between the ages of eighteen and twenty-four. Every indication is that they are registering overwhelmingly as Democrats, even in suburban counties where their parents are Republican.* According to an in-depth Gallup Poll that formed the basis for a *Newsweek* cover story in October, 1971, 38 per cent of these new voters considered themselves Democrats, 18 per cent considered themselves Republicans, and a stunning 42 per cent called themselves independent, usually to the left of the Democrats. And this survey included noncollege, working-class youth. In fact, of the new voters, only a third are collegians; the greater number are now working—or, if they are in the armed forces, will soon be working—in the plants, factories, and offices of America. Rather than abandoning these noncollege young voters to the Right, we believe progressive Democrats *who will talk*

* Three million new voters have already registered. If only half of the 25 million between eighteen and twenty-four vote for president in 1972, and two-thirds vote Democratic, Nixon would lose nine states he carried in 1968. These nine states represent 150 electoral votes, and include California, Ohio, Illinois, and New Jersey.

about gut economic issues can draw their support. These voters, unlike their college counterparts, already have families and mortgages. Hard talk about the cost of food, and electricity, and bank loans, and taxes may reach directly into this group's foremost concerns; and it is on issues like these that Nixon is most vulnerable.

If Phillips has left the new voters out of his equations, his enthusiasm for the southern strategy has also blinded him to the increasing registration of blacks in the South. This new black vote was decisive in the Georgia and Florida elections in 1970, and, as more blacks register every month, they will become a long-term force in southern politics. Together with the new eighteen-year-old voters, they may well be a key factor in liberalizing the South.

In his passion for ethnicity and geography, Phillips also overlooks the purely nonideological factors that often tend to decide elections: for one, money, and for another, how the candidate performs on television. Such variables help such ideologically different politicians as John Lindsay, William Brock, Jay Rockefeller, and Ronald Reagan equally.

In short, there is no evidence that Richard Nixon is fashioning a new permanent majority or inaugurating a new era. He is a minority president, elected with 43 per cent of the vote. In 1968, and again in 1970, he failed to elect a Republican majority in either chamber. (The GOP lost nine House seats in 1970.) Meanwhile, most governorships are held by Democrats. And, according to all the polls, more people today think of themselves as independents or as Democrats, than as Republicans. The Gallup Poll released in October, 1971 showed that, for the first time in thirty years, the Democrats now command a majority among business and professional people: 34 per cent to 31 per cent, with 39 per cent independent. The same survey revealed that among "manual workers," the split was 48 per cent Democrats, 19 per cent Republican, and 33 per cent independent. Among blacks, it was 72 per cent Democrats, 9 per cent Republican, and 19 per cent independent. (In 1960, 23 per cent of blacks described themselves as Republicans.)

These figures, when coupled with the data on new eighteen-year-old and black enrollments, suggest there simply is no such thing as an "emerging Republican majority."

The Real Majority is less substantial, but it is pinned on the same premises as Phillips's book. Scammon and Wattenberg are for the most part interested in tactics and technique. Their vision ends with getting elected. (The last chapter, in fact, is written like a textbook for ambitious politicians, telling them what to say, what not to say.)

The thesis of the book is that the young will vote like their parents, the Left is small, the average voters is "unyoung, unpoor, and unblack," and so the Democrats had better talk tough about the "Social Issue" if they want to win elections. By the "Social Issue," Scammon and Wattenberg mean an ambiguous mixture of campus unrest, black militancy, crime, drugs, and the general decline of Puritan morality—everything from Weathermen to pubic hair. In a typical contrived litany, in which the juxtapositions are stunning, Scammon and Wattenberg write: "Most voters felt they gained little from crime, or integration, or wild kids, or new values, or dissent."

But nowhere in the book's 305 pages are there any ideas about how to go about actually solving social ills. The point is to get the vote of the middle-aged, middle-class, Middle America voter by tough talk, and forget about improving his life. The distressing assumption behind this book is that *campaigning* is more important than *governing*. Issues are not to be faced and resolved; they are to be manipulated, used as tools to secure votes. So the authors tell politicians how to slide around an issue:

Do *NOT* say: "Well, I don't agree with Students for a Demo-

cratic Society when they invade a college President's office, but I understand their deep sense of frustration."
   DO say: "When students break laws they will be treated as lawbreakers."

But as for serious thoughts about how to stop crime, or end the war, or communicate with the young, Scammon and Wattenberg have nothing to offer. They accept the essential ideas of Kevin Phillips, and try to deal with them by opportunism and cleverness, thereby reducing all of politics to gamesmanship. The advice they offer—and the ideological biases they never admit to, but consistently reveal—is what one might expect from counselors to Lyndon Johnson, Hubert Humphrey, and Senator Henry Jackson.
   The Real Majority enjoyed a brief fling on the Great American Hype Machine, and many pols embraced it as a bible during the 1970 campaign. The Vice President, under the influence of the book, traveled around the country trying to connect the most moderate Democrats—like Harrison Williams and Joseph Montoya—to violence, crime, and smut. In the last week of the campaign, the President himself went on the road, making ranting speeches against "terrorists and thugs," denouncing "ugly demonstrators of the far Left."
   The President's advance men began intentionally to let a few hecklers into each rally as props. When a single pebble was thrown at the President in Vermont, it became "rocks" in a speech the next night. In San Jose, California, the President climbed on the hood of his car and flashed a V-sign to antiwar demonstrators in order to provoke them; as he said, "That's what they hate to see."
   It was a conscious tactic to run a national campaign against scapegoats and straw men, to exaggerate and create disorder, and then blame the out-of-power Democrats for that disorder. It was a vulgarization of the Scammon and Wattenberg thesis. And it did not work.
   George Murphy, Max Rafferty, Nelson Gross, and Ralph

Smith were badly beaten. The Republicans lost nine House seats and eleven governorships. And the liberals who refused to hitch their campaigns to the Social Issue—Gilligan, Hart, Muskie, Kennedy, and Proxmire—all won. Agnew began to lose strength and credibility. Muskie had his finest hour with his quiet election-eve appeal to reason. Unemployment, job security, pensions, taxes, inflation—concrete economic interests—proved to have a deeper hold on the country than the fears manufactured by politicians. They can do so again. That's what this manifesto is all about.

That the new populism is both morally and intellectually imperative at this desperate time in history is clear to us. But more to the point, we also think a new populist thrust is *politically* appropriate, that such a strategy has a strong *practical* chance of success.

One reason we have already mentioned: the 11 million eighteen- to twenty-one-year-olds enfranchised by the 26th Amendment, and the 14 million more between twenty-one and twenty-four who were ineligible to vote in 1968. Together, this amounts to 25 million new voters, or almost one-third of all the votes cast in 1968; and in that election, Richard Nixon was elected president with fewer votes than he had when he lost in 1960. If the Gallup survey holds, the bulk of this group would lean leftward. And another 16 million eighteen-year-olds will be able to vote in 1976.

There is also the growing proportion of black voters. As it is, the over-all black population has increased from 18.9 million in 1960, to 22.6 million in 1970. And at least a million new black voters have been registered in the South alone. The black vote is concentrated in the pivotal electoral states—2.2 million in New York, 1.4 million in California, and 1.4 million in Illinois. Will that vote go along with a populist movement? We think it will, and one indication is that black leaders like Rev. Jesse Jackson, Julian Bond, and Congressmen Ron Dellums and John Conyers are urging a populist alliance with low-incomes whites, while the voices of black separatism seem to be diminishing.

But there are also signs outside of electoral politics that a new populism might be next on the agenda of national consciousness.

The most dramatic sign is the immense credibility, popularity, and political clout of Ralph Nader. More than anyone else, Nader has created a public consciousness of corporate crime, and a national consumer mood and movement to rectify these crimes.* Along with his muckraking Raiders, Nader has produced twenty reports and has already forced Congress to pass the Auto Safety Act of 1966, the Wholesome Meat Act of 1967, the Coal Mine Health and Safety Act of 1969, plus substantial reforms of the FDA and the FTC. Nader has also founded four new institutions—the Center for the Study of Responsive Law, the Public Interest Research Group, the Corporate Accountability Research Group, and the Center for Auto Safety. He is the model modern populist —urban, fact-filled, unflamboyant, and skilled in his use of the mass media.

Another populist portent is the steady growth of John Gardner's Common Cause. In its first year, this activist organization recruited 215,000 members—mostly white, mostly middle class—who paid a minimum of $15 in annual dues. Common Cause has a staff of fifty, plus several hundred volunteers. So far, it has helped lobby for passage of the 26th Amendment, helped defeat the SST, and filed law suits to limit campaign spending and open up voter registration procedures.

In Denver, an organizing effort funded by Common Cause and called the Colorado Project has built a coalition of unions (the UAW and the Steelworkers), farmers, white-

---

* One indication of this new consciousness is that the anticorporate broadside *America, Inc.*, by Norton Mintz and Jerry Cohen, has been on the best-seller list for months.

collar professionals, Chicanos, and students. The Project has been crusading for tax reform and against the utility and insurance companies. The 70,000-member state AFL-CIO, having voted to endorse the program, is assessing members 8 cents a month to help finance it and enlisting them in efforts to place several initiatives on the ballot.

The Colorado Project, directed by Craig Barnes and David Mixner, has already waged a partially successful campaign against an $11.3 million gas and electricity rate increase sought by the state-wide utility monopoly. Only half the request was approved, and the monopoly was ordered to limit its spending in areas the Project had cited as "abuses to the taxpayers"—advertising, consultants' fees (sometimes $500 a day), propaganda films, country club dues for executives—as well as to stop charging special low rates to corporate customers.

White ethnic workingmen are also starting to organize for social reform. In Lake County, Indiana, where unemployment is rising in the steel mills, 142 community organizations have united to form the Calumet Community Congress (CCC). At the founding convention of the Congress last year, the keynote speaker was John Esposito, an assistant to Ralph Nader, who blasted U.S. Steel for its "unjust enrichment at the cost of the health and safety of the workers of America's biggest company town—Gary, Indiana."

The next day, Lake County Democratic boss, John Krupa, called the new ethnic organization, "an alien group . . . at the root of the CCC is the godless, atheistic force of communism."

In Washington last June, another new national ethnic organization had its founding convention. It is called PIGS —standing for Poles, Italians, Germans, and Slavs. PIGS, funded by the Urban Coalition and the Center for Urban Ethnic Affairs, is trying to organize around local issues —poverty funds, local health centers, and preservation of neighborhoods against expressways and high-rise housing.

In Detroit, the Black-Polish Conference has been in existence for two years. In Newark, Stephen Adubato, running on a platform of ethnic pride and cooperation with blacks, has won control of the North Ward Democratic Party away from Anthony Imperiale, the champion of white vigilanteeism. In Milwaukee, Father James Groppi, who led civil rights marches five years ago, has come back to his old run-down neighborhood, and is now organizing Italians for populist goals. In New York City, the city-wide Congress of Italian-American Organizations (CIAO), led by Mary Sansone, has fought for day care centers and city funds for senior-citizen programs in Italian neighborhoods.

The potential strength of a political movement based on economic justice for this "conservative" constituency is underscored by the severe pocketbook pressures afflicting white ethnic neighborhoods. Between 1969 and 1971, welfare payments to white neighborhoods increased 60 per cent faster than those to mostly black and Puerto Rican communities: a measure, in large part, of the inability of white adults to maintain the tradition of supporting their elderly parents. And desertion by fathers—a classic symptom of an "underclass" lifestyle—is beginning to emerge in Italian and Jewish neighborhoods. These symptoms of economic distress suggest a fertile field for a class-based political movement.

All these groups are symptoms of a stirring of the white working class, of a movement that is a complex mix of ethnicity and economics. Says Msgr. Geno Baroni, the director of the Center for Urban Ethnic Affairs: "Nobody has done anything for the white working class since Social Security. Today there is a budding national movement of white workers wonderfully parallel to where the blacks were a few years ago. My hunch is that this one is going to move even faster."

And finally, there are now large segments of the AFL-CIO that have recognized the Vietnam War to be a monstrous folly, and that seem open to populist ideas and coalitions.

Last February, when a conference of antiwar students, professors, and union leaders was convened at Harvard, some of labor's best men attended: Leonard Woodcock of the UAW; Harold Gibbons, international vice president of the Teamsters; Cleveland Robinson, president of the Distributive Workers of America; and Jack Potofsky, president of the Amalgamated Clothing Workers. In addition, there is now liberal leadership of the Oil, Chemical and Atomic Workers Union, in many locals of the United Steelworkers, and in the state AFL-CIO in Colorado, Virginia, California, and Texas.

These trends, we believe, point the way to an effective political coalition for the 1970's: the traditional liberalism of intellectuals and racial minorities, the new voting strength of the young, and the economic concerns of labor unions and white ethnic Americans. A political movement that fuses these elements in an attack on economic privilege can build a new political majority based neither on fear nor on dreams but on the demand for fairness and justice.

★ A Final Word

In this manifesto, we have outlined a *political* program and proposed a *political* strategy. In a time when politics offers the rhetoric of redemption and revolution at the drop of a press release, we emphasize the limits of a political effort. This is not a summons to Utopia. It is not a call to revolution.

We are talking instead about what is possible in this generation, in our time; we are talking about a political movement that takes money and power from some people, and redistributes it to other groups. This is a limited idea. If all our proposals were adopted next year—or next week—there would still be cancer, and sexual frustration, and boredom, and loneliness. All of the frailties endemic to the human condition would still be very much with us.

We can give some sense of who would suffer from the ideas we offer. Clearly, stockholders would have less money from their holdings. The top 5 to 20 per cent income-earners and wealth-holders would find their tax bills sharply increased; and summer homes and European vacations would be more difficult to achieve. Some respected citizens would be indicted and convicted of criminal offenses—the kind that don't show up on police blotters, but that do take money out of the pockets of millions of us, and that do threaten the health and lives of many of us.

General Motors wouldn't be nearly as big and powerful as it is today; the Rockefeller Foundation would have less money to do "good works" with, since its taxes would be higher. If Harvard or Columbia wanted to expand its facilities at the expense of a black or Italian or Jewish neighboring community, that neighborhood would have the clear legal right —and the legal and professional talent—to fight that expansion; so students and professors might have to use outmoded equipment and crowded spaces. Craft unions wouldn't be allowed to keep out blacks or hold down the labor supply, and they might feel their economic security jeopardized. Congressmen would be under far closer scrutiny than they are now; and business and professional people would be eating a lot fewer expense account meals.

That's a lot of people to antagonize; although we believe, perhaps too naively, that many people would accept an end to *their* special favor or fix, if they could believe that "the fix" was ending for the other guy. This sense of political fairness, in fact, is a basic reason for a populist movement. A redistribution of power and wealth will certainly not bring full economic equality, nor do we believe that such a world is possible or desirable, except in the most Utopian sense. But the rebirth of a sense of fairness in our economic and political system—the revival of such "radical" notions as that the law applies to rich and poor, to powerful and powerless alike, and that the possibility for access to a better life is in fact a real possibility—would begin to reverse the steady loss of faith and trust that has afflicted our society. Clearly those most hurt are those with the power to fight hardest against the ideas we stand for. That is what makes it so important to build the broadest, toughest coalition we can in the time ahead. Because while a new populism will not mean Nirvana or the Final Triumph of Virtue, it can make life a little more humane for a majority of our countrymen. Nothing more. But nothing less either.